Grade 3

Treasures

W9-BEY-172

Practice
Book
B

Macmillan
McGraw-Hill

The McGraw-Hill Companies

Mc Graw Hill **Macmillan**
McGraw-Hill

Published by Macmillan/McGraw-Hill, of McGraw-Hill Education, a division of The McGraw-Hill Companies, Inc.,
Two Penn Plaza, New York, New York 10121.

Printed in the United States of America

12 13 ROV 15 14

Contents

Unit 2 • Discoveries

© Macmillan/McGraw-Hill

Unit 3 • Opportunities

Unit 4 • Choices

© Macmillan/McGraw-Hill

Unit 5 • Challenges

Unit 6 • Achievements

Name _____

**The vocabulary words are in italics in the story below.
Read the story and answer the questions.**

My First Day in a New House

RRRR-ING! When the alarm rang I *fumbled* to shut it off. I didn't
know where it was at first. This was the first day in our new house. I shut
off the alarm clock and *trudged* down the hall to take a shower. After I got
dressed I went *downstairs* to have breakfast.

"Well," I told my mother, "today is my first day in a new school. I am
a little *nervous* about going." "That's *nonsense*, Jenna," Mom *chuckled*.
"You will still be going to the same school. We moved only two blocks
from our old house!"

1. What is Jenna *clumsy* with?

_____

2. How did Jenna walk down the hallway to the shower?

_____

3. Why does Jenna go *downstairs*?

_____

4. What is Jenna worried about?

_____

5. What does Mom think is foolish?

_____

6. Use two of the vocabulary words in one sentence about Jenna.

_____

_____

Make up a new story. Complete the story frame below by filling in names of characters, descriptions of a setting, and important events in the beginning, middle, and end. Use the elements in parentheses to complete each blank.

(character) _____'s First Day At

(setting) _____

It was a (setting) _____ day. (character)

_____ was feeling (character's feeling) _____

about going to (setting) _____. It didn't help when

(important event) _____. Now the time had come.

(character) _____ set off for (setting) _____.

All week (character) _____ had been thinking about

this moment. (Character) _____ walked to the (setting)

_____. The (setting) _____ was (important

event) _____. (Character) _____ could not

believe it and felt (character's feeling) _____. So after

some thinking, (character) _____ began to (important

event) _____. After a minute, (important event)

_____. Then (character) _____

(important event) _____. Finally, (character)

_____ was at (setting) _____ and

(important event) _____.

At Home: Ask your child to tell you the characters, setting, and plot of the story he or she wrote.

As you read *First Day Jitters*, fill in the Story Map.

```
┌─────────────────────────────────────────────────┐
│                                                   │
│              Characters                           │
│                                                   │
└─────────────────────────────────────────────────┘

┌─────────────────────────────────────────────────┐
│                                                   │
│              Setting                              │
│                                                   │
└─────────────────────────────────────────────────┘

┌─────────────────────────────────────────────────┐
│                                                   │
│              Beginning                            │
│                                                   │
└─────────────────────────────────────────────────┘
                      │
                      ▼
┌─────────────────────────────────────────────────┐
│                                                   │
│              Middle                               │
│                                                   │
└─────────────────────────────────────────────────┘
                      │
                      ▼
┌─────────────────────────────────────────────────┐
│                                                   │
│              End                                  │
│                                                   │
└─────────────────────────────────────────────────┘
```

How does the information you wrote in this Story Map help you
analyze story structure in *First Day Jitters*?

At Home: Have your child use the chart to retell the story.

First Day Jitters • Book 3.1/Unit 1   ◇ 3

As I read, I will pay attention to punctuation.

	"Come on, lazy bones! What are you doing inside on this
11	beautiful day?" Mom said, as she walked into Nicky's room.
21	Nicky was lying on her bed, turning the pages of a
32	magazine. She looked up at her mother and sighed.
41	"What's there to do?" she asked.
47	"Let's hop in the car and go explore our new town," said
59	Mom. She watched as Nicky rolled slowly off the bed.
69	Then they both headed downstairs.
74	"I can't believe we have to drive every time we want to
86	buy something!" Nicky said. "I used to be able to walk to
98	all the stores by myself!"
103	Mom nodded her head a little sadly. "I know this is very
115	different from living in the city. It will take awhile for us to
128	get used to being in a new place, but maybe this little town
141	will surprise us." 144

Comprehension Check

1. How do you think Nicky feels about living in a new town? **Make Inferences**

2. What advice does Nicky's mom give her? **Plot**

	Words Read	−	Number of Errors	=	Words Correct Score
First Read		−		=	
Second Read		−		=	

 At Home: Help your child read the passage, paying attention to the goal at the top of the page.

Read Bar Graph 1. Use the information from Bar Graph 1 to complete Bar Graph 2.

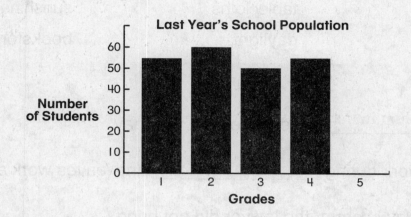

Show the correct number of students in each grade for the new school year if the population changed as follows.

1. Grade 3 increased by 5 students.

2. Grade 1 has 10 fewer students than last year.

3. Grade 2 has the same number of students.

4. Grade 4 has 5 more students.

5. This year Grade 5 moved into the school with 45 students.

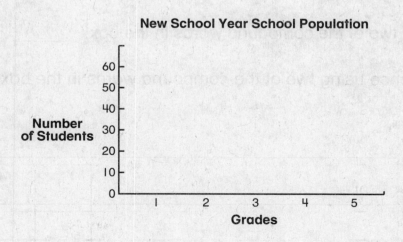

At Home: Ask your child to add the number of students in his or her class to Bar Graph 2.

First Day Jitters • Book 3.I/Unit I   5

© Macmillan/McGraw-Hill

Fill in the blank with a compound word from the box.

anything	tablecloths	sunshine
birthday	daylight	bookstore

1. The _____ welcomed the new day.

2. Kyle starts work during _____ and leaves work at night.

3. On her first day in court, the lawyer did not bring _____ to eat.

4. On opening day the restaurant had all new _____ for the tables.

5. To celebrate my _____, my parents gave me a new puppy.

6. After my first day of school I went to the _____.

7. Create a new compound word using the first small word and second

   small word of two of the compound words in the box. _____

8. Write a sentence using two of the compound words in the box at the top
   of the page.

   _____

   _____

At Home: Look for compound words in newspaper or magazine articles. Have your child tell you what they mean.

Name _____

Complete each list with words with short vowel sounds.

Short *a* sound

_____
_____
_____
_____
_____
_____

Short *e* sound

_____
_____
_____
_____
_____
_____

Short *i* sound

_____
_____
_____
_____
_____
_____

Short *o* sound

_____
_____
_____
_____
_____

Short *u* sound

_____
_____
_____
_____
_____

At Home: Work with your child to name two-syllable words that have short vowel sounds in each syllable, such as rabbit, practice, and finish.

Name _____

Use the clues to fill in the crossword puzzle.

crackle   announced   soared   starry   envelope   photograph

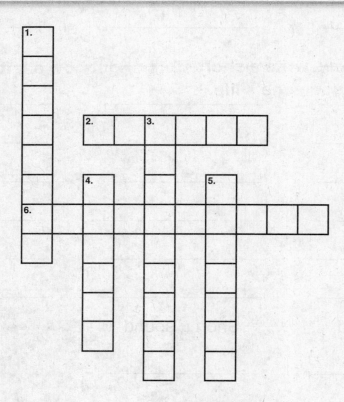

ACROSS

2. what the night sky looks like

6. picture in an album

DOWN

1. usually contains a letter

3. said in a formal way

4. flew through the sky

5. a noisy snapping sound

© Macmillan/McGraw-Hill

Name _____

The **characters** are the people and animals in a story. The **setting** is where and when the story takes place. The **plot** is the important events in the beginning, middle, and end of the story.

On the lines below, write a short story about how a letter or an e-mail changed someone's life.

_____

_____

_____

_____

_____

_____

_____

_____

_____

_____

_____

_____

_____

At Home: Ask your child to choose one character mentioned in the story and tell what he or she thinks about the character and why.

Dear Juno • **Book 3.1/Unit I**   9

As you read *Dear Juno*, fill in the Character Web.

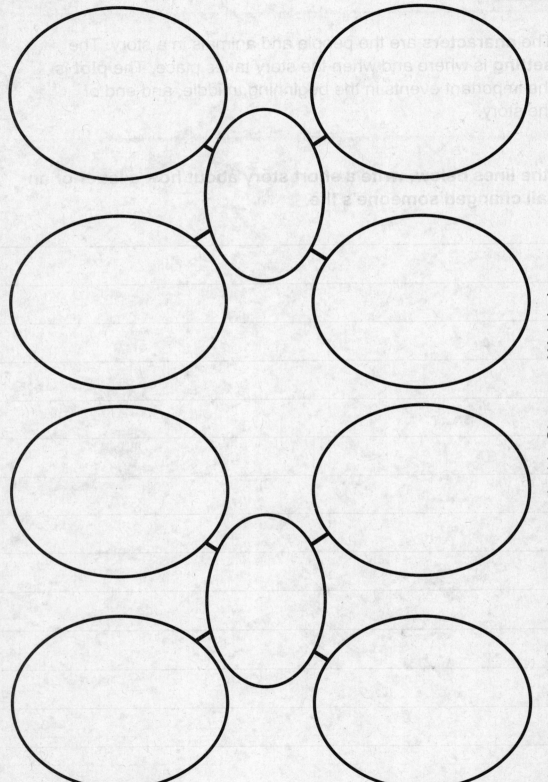

How does the information you wrote in this Character Web help you analyze story structure in *Dear Juno*?

At Home: Have your child use the chart to retell the story.

As I read, I will pay attention to the dialogue and punctuation.

	For the past three weeks, ever since his family moved
10	to Seward, Alaska, the fog had barely lifted. It matched
20	Sam's gloomy mood.
23	"Sam, why don't you go out and play?" coaxed
32	his mom.
34	Sam wiped the sun off the window and dried his hand
45	on his blue jeans. He grabbed a couple of cookies and
56	went to sit on the porch steps. Playing was the last thing
68	he felt like doing. Why did Dad have to lose his job?
80	His father used to be a dockworker. When he couldn't
90	find another job, he announced that it was time to move.
101	"There are good jobs in Alaska," he told Sam and his
112	mom one evening. Soon after, Sam's dad landed a job
122	working on a fishing boat in Seward. 129

Comprehension Check

1. Why does Sam feel gloomy? **Draw Conclusions**

2. Why did Sam's family move to Alaska? **Plot**

	Words Read	−	Number of Errors	=	Words Correct Score
First Read		−		=	
Second Read		−		=	

At Home: Help your child read the passage, paying attention to the goal at the top of the page.

Use the information in the paragraph below to complete the time line. Then answer the questions below about your completed time line.

Some Important Dates in Computer History

Computers have changed the way people all over the world communicate. Over the years, there have been many inventions and improvements related to computers. The first Electronic Numerical Integrator and Calculator computer was built in 1946. It was called ENIAC. Another famous computer called UNIVAC I was first used by the U.S. Census Bureau in 1951. But, could computers really think? In 1956 people started to wonder. That's when a computer first beat a human in a game of chess. Computer use continued to grow. In 1969 the U.S. Department of Defense created a computer network known as ARPANET. Of course we all know computers are used for games as well. It was in 1972 that the video game "Pong" was introduced by Nolan Bushnell.

1945   1950   1955   1960   1965   1970   1975

1. How many years after ENIAC was built was Pong introduced?

_____

2. About 7 years after Pong was introduced, the game Pac-Man was sold in Japan. In what year did this event happen?

_____

© Macmillan/McGraw-Hill

At Home: Ask your child to make up another question to answer using the time line. Have your child explain how the time line answers that question.

Use the words in the box to complete the letter. Use context clues in the sentences to help find the correct word.

conductor	orchestra	cymbal	percussion
snare drum	triangle	kettledrum	

Dear Manny,

How are you? How is your family? I hope everyone is well. I am good. Yesterday my class went on a field trip. My class went to hear a concert performed by our town's _____. The musicians knew exactly when they were supposed to play. The _____ stood in front of them with his baton in his hand and directed their playing. There were many different _____ instruments that were played by being hit or shaken. There were several kinds of drums, including a small double-headed drum called a _____ because of the snares across its lower head. It made a sound like a rattle when it was played. I liked the drum that looked like a giant covered soup bowl. It is called a _____.

There were other instruments, too. The brass _____ is shaped like a plate, but I can't imagine eating my dinner on it! To play it you strike it with a stick or even with another instrument just like it. I think the _____ has the funniest name of all. It makes me think of shapes we study in school.

What have you been up to? How is everybody at school? Tell them I said hello. Write to me soon.

Your friend,
James

At Home: Ask your child to tell you the definitions of the words in the box.

© Macmillan/McGraw-Hill

Name _____

**A. Match the syllable from Column A with a syllable with the long
vowel sound from Column B to form words. Write the word.**

Column A	Column B	Column C
1. re	rade	1. _____
2. enve	plete	2. _____
3. air	cline	3. _____
4. pa	prise	4. _____
5. com	plane	5. _____
6. sur	fuse	6. _____
7. de	lope	7. _____

B. Use three of the words you made above in sentences.

8. _____

_____

9. _____

_____

10. _____

_____

© Macmillan/McGraw-Hill

At Home: Ask your child to name other two- or three-
syllable words that have at least one syllable that contains a
vowel, consonant, and final *e* pattern.

Some of the words below have more than one meaning.
Check a dictionary to be sure you know all the meanings of each
word. Then write a story using all of the vocabulary words. You
only need to use one meaning of each word.

> neighborhood   content   addressing   resort

_____

_____

_____

_____

_____

_____

_____

_____

_____

_____

_____

> A **main idea** is the major, or most important, point that a writer makes. **Supporting details** are details that reinforce the main idea.

Read the passage, then list the main idea and supporting details.

Suppose you are going out to help with the community garden. It is a very hot day. What should you do to take care of yourself? It is important to drink water and take breaks if you are going to be in the sun for a long time. When you spend a lot of time in the sun, your body loses water. This can make you very tired because your body needs water to function properly. Even if you are not thirsty, drink some water before you go out. Bring more water with you. Also be sure to take a break after an hour or two. Walk to the nearest shady tree and sit down. Drink some of the water you brought with you. It is important to be careful when you spend time in the hot sun.

Main Idea: _____

_____

Supporting Detail: _____

_____

Supporting Detail: _____

_____

Supporting Detail: _____

_____

At Home: Ask your child to tell you the main idea and three supporting details of a book he or she has read recently.

Name _____

As you read *Whose Habitat Is It?*, fill in the Main Idea Web.

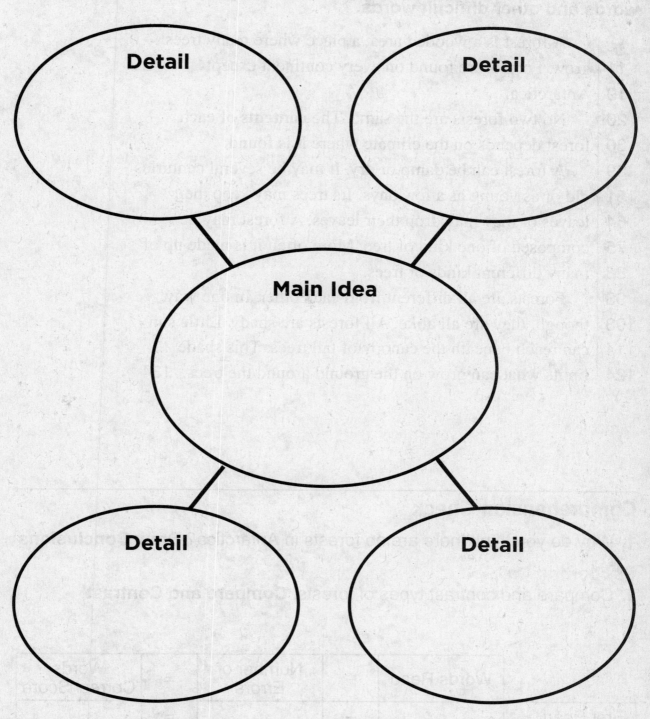

Detail

Detail

Main Idea

Detail

Detail

How does the information you wrote in this Main Idea Web help you summarize *Whose Habitat Is It?*

 At Home: Have your child use the chart to retell the story.

As I read, I will pay attention to my pronunciation of vocabulary words and other difficult words.

	A forest is a wooded area, a place where many trees
11	grow. Forests are found on every continent except
19	Antarctica.
20	No two forests are the same. The **contents** of each
30	forest depends on the climate where it is found.
39	A forest can be damp or dry. It may be several centuries
51	old or as young as a few days. Its trees may keep their
64	leaves or they may drop their leaves. A forest may be
75	composed of one kind of tree. More often it is made up of
88	many different kinds of trees.
93	Forests are all different from each other. In one way,
103	though, they are all alike. All forests are shady. Little sun
114	can reach beneath the canopy of tall trees. This shade
124	limits what can grow on the ground around the trees. 134

Comprehension Check

1. Why do you think there are no forests in Antarctica? **Draw Conclusions**

2. Compare and contrast types of forests. **Compare and Contrast**

	Words Read	–	Number of Errors	=	Words Correct Score
First Read		–		=	
Second Read		–		=	

© Macmillan/McGraw-Hill

At Home: Help your child read the passage, paying attention to the goal at the top of the page.

Name _____

Listed below are some words to define. Write down the steps you will take to find the words in the dictionary. Then define each word and use it in a sentence.

Step 1. Look at the first letter of the word.

Step 2. _____

Step 3. _____

1. recognize _____

_____

2. munch _____

_____

3. attempt _____

_____

4. conservation _____

_____

5. threaten _____

_____

6. mention _____

_____

At Home: Have your child look up unfamiliar words as he or she reads a favorite book.

Whose Habitat Is It?
Book 3.I/Unit I

◇ 19

**Use a dictionary to find the meanings of the words below. Then
fill in the blanks with the right word.**

deforms	expanse	feeble	massive
native	phenomenon	represents	swarms

Antarctica is a large _____ of land that has water all around

it. One winter _____ is the increased amount of sea ice. The

ice _____ about 90 percent of all the ice in the world. The

winter sun is too _____ to melt the sea ice. The ice is so

heavy that it _____ the South Pole. That is why Earth is a bit

pear-shaped. The most _____ iceberg ever spotted was the

size of the country Belgium. Under the sea ice, _____ of

small fish called krill feed on algae. The extreme cold and ice mean there

are only two _____ species of flowers in Antarctica.

At Home: Ask your child to tell you at least two meanings
that he or she found for each word listed above when looking
up the word in a dictionary.

Name _____

Use the following words with the long *a* sound to write a poem on any topic you choose. The poem does not have to rhyme at the ends of lines. A poem's rhyme can also be a rhyming sound in the middle of the word.

plain	paint	sway	braid	tray
plays	bay	gray	May	ray

_____

_____

_____

_____

_____

_____

_____

_____

_____

_____

_____

_____

At Home: Have a family contest to see who can create the most words with the long *a* sound using the blends *ai* or *ay*.

Name _____

| down | echoes | huddle | fierce |
| junior | shuffles | whips | |

Write a paragraph about a trip someone takes. Use each of the vocabulary words in the box in your paragraph.

_____

_____

_____

_____

_____

_____

_____

_____

_____

_____

_____

_____

_____

Read the article below. Circle the main idea and underline the supporting details in the article. Then use the information to write a main idea statement and its supporting details.

The weather at Antarctica's South Pole presents special challenges for humans. During the six months of summer, the sun never sets. All of that sun can be dangerous. The South Pole is at a high altitude, so the sunlight is more intense. The sun also reflects off the snow. Everyone must wear sunglasses outdoors all the time. Some people get sunburn on their eyes. This condition is called snow blindness.

The cold is another danger. In winter, the temperature averages about –76 degrees Fahrenheit (-60 degrees Celsius). The cold temperatures mean people are at risk of frostbite and sickness from the cold.

The South Pole gets less than 4 mm of rain or snow a month. The Sahara gets about the same amount. Even though it's cold, the South Pole is a desert environment. The dry air creates the risk of cracked and bleeding skin. People protect their skin with petroleum jelly and cream.

Now write your main idea statement.

_____

_____

Write the details that support your main idea statement.

_____

_____

_____

At Home: Ask your child to write a news story about something that happened during his or her day. Have your child point out the main idea and supporting details.

As you read _Penguin Chick_, fill in the Main Idea Chart.

Main Idea	Details

How does the information you wrote in this Main Idea Chart help you summarize _Penguin Chick_?

At Home: Have your child use the chart to retell the story.

As I read, I will pay attention to tempo.

	If you travel the waters of Antarctica on a fishing vessel,
11	you might spy a great white bird circling your boat. And it
23	might be the magnificent wandering albatross. It's the
31	largest of all sea birds, and it does indeed wander. It spends
43	most of its life in the air, flying over southern seas. It's a
56	true sea bird. It even sleeps on top of the water! Early
68	sailors thought the albatross was a sign of good luck.
78	When one followed their ship, it meant they would have
88	good winds.
90	If you should see an albatross with dark wing tips then
101	you know it's a junior bird. An adult albatross has mainly
112	white wing feathers. At either age, a wandering albatross
121	is a graceful bird. It has long, narrow wings, a long neck,
133	and a yellow-pink bill. 138

Comprehension Check

1. Why do you think the albatross is called a wandering albatross? **Draw Conclusions**

2. Compare and contrast an adult albatross and a junior albatross. **Compare and Contrast**

	Words Read	–	Number of Errors	=	Words Correct Score
First Read		–		=	
Second Read		–		=	

At Home: Help your child read the passage, paying attention to the goal at the top of the page.

Penguin Chick • **Book 3.1/Unit 1**   25

Name _____

Just as music has a rhythm, so does poetry. The rhythm of a poem comes from the mix of accented and unaccented syllables. The **rhythmic pattern** in "Antarctic Anthem" relies on the repeating accents of the word *Antarctica.* Also found in poetry is **imagery** which is the use of words to create a vivid picture in the reader's mind.

Choose a familiar song such as "Mary Had a Little Lamb" or "Twinkle, Twinkle, Little Star." Using the same rhythm of that song, make up a new poem about a place you have visited. If you want, you can invent silly words, such as park-tica and New York-tica to complete your rhymes. Make sure you use imagery to create a picture of the place in the reader's mind.

_____

_____

_____

_____

_____

_____

_____

_____

At Home: Read aloud a few favorite poems with your child to get a feel for the rhythmic patterns.

A **homograph** is a word that has more than one meaning. The word is always spelled the same.

For example, the word *down* can mean two different things.

The chicks' <u>down</u> was replaced with feathers as it aged.

Sam came <u>down</u> the street on his new scooter.

The following words are homographs. For each one, write two questions, beginning with What is . . . , that show the different meanings of the words. Then work with a partner to see if you know all the meanings.

1. slip _____

_____

_____

2. date _____

_____

_____

3. steer _____

_____

_____

© Macmillan/McGraw-Hill

At Home: Select other common homographs and write
questions for them. Then play a few rounds of the game with
the whole family

Penguin Chick • **Book 3.1/Unit I**   **27**

Name _____

Each word below makes the long *o* sound. Think of a rhyming word; it doesn't have to be spelled the same way. Then write a two-line rhyming poem, using the two words.

1. float _____

Poem: _____

_____

2. sold _____

Poem: _____

_____

3. show _____

Poem: _____

_____

4. toast _____

Poem: _____

_____

5. grown _____

Poem: _____

_____

At Home: Write a poem together using at least ten words with the long *o* sound.

Name _____

A. Write the vocabulary word that fits each meaning, filling in one letter on each blank.

1. having nothing wrong   __ __ Ⓞ __ __ Ⓞ __

2. a wish to eat   __ __ __ __ __ Ⓞ __ __ __

3. to meet a need   __ __ __ __ Ⓞ __ __ __

4. to be able to do   __ __ __ Ⓞ __ __ __ __

5. a task needing effort   Ⓞ __ __ __ __ __ __ __ __ __

6. full of strength and energy   Ⓞ __ __ __ __ __ __ __ __

B. Now rearrange the circled letters to form a word that fits into both places in the sentence below.

7. Cats _____ the furniture, so let's

_____ off a cat from our list.

You are going to write a story about someone named Linda.
Circle the choice you want for each item below. Then write a
story using the items you circled.

Problem: Linda wanted to:

get a pet   train the family dog   enter her dog in a dog show

Character: Linda was:

clever   funny   confused

Solution: To solve her problem, Linda:

worked by herself worked with friends worked with a teacher

_____

_____

_____

_____

_____

_____

_____

_____

_____

_____

_____

© Macmillan/McGraw-Hill

At Home: Together, make up stories about characters that
have a problem and take steps to solve it. Make up funny
stories or science-fiction stories.

Name _____

As you read *The Perfect Pet*, fill in the Problem and Solution Chart.

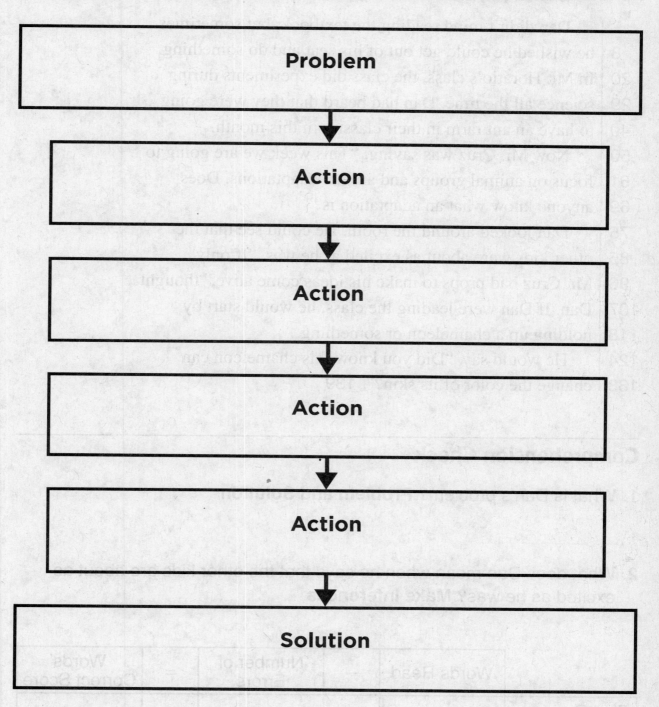

Problem

↓

Action

↓

Action

↓

Action

↓

Action

↓

Solution

How does the information you wrote in this Problem and Solution Chart help you analyze story structure in *The Perfect Pet*?

At Home: Have your child use the chart to retell the story.

As I read, I will pay attention to punctuation.

	Dan didn't mind reading the textbook, but sometimes
8	he wished he could get out of his seat and do something.
20	In Mr. Horatio's class, the class did experiments during
29	science all the time. Dan had heard that they were going
40	to have an ant farm in their classroom this month.
50	Now Mr. Cruz was saying, "This week we are going to
61	focus on animal groups and animal adaptations. Does
69	anyone know what an adaptation is?"
75	Dan looked around the room. He could see that the
85	other kids were about as excited as he was. "If only
96	Mr. Cruz had props to make his ideas come alive," thought
107	Dan. If Dan were leading the class, he would start by
118	holding up a chameleon or something.
124	He would say, "Did you know this chameleon can
133	change the color of its skin?" 139

Comprehension Check

1. What is Dan's problem? **Problem and Solution**

2. What does Dan mean when he says that the other kids are about as excited as he was? **Make Inferences**

	Words Read	–	Number of Errors	=	Words Correct Score
First Read		–		=	
Second Read		–		=	

© Macmillan/McGraw-Hill

At Home: Help your child read the passage, paying attention to the goal at the top of the page.

Label the body parts of the bird.

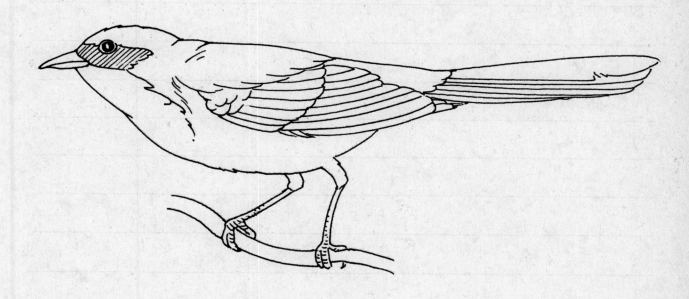

At Home: Help your child draw a diagram of something other than an animal. The objective is not drawing but to show an understanding of creating diagrams.

The Perfect Pet • **Book 3.1/Unit 1**   33

◇ **Practice**

Vocabulary Strategy:
Multiple-Meaning
Words

Name _____

Use the word *catch* or another multiple-meaning word. Create a dictionary entry for the word. Remember to include:

- Entry Word

- Parts of Speech

- Numbers for Different Meanings

- Examples of Word in Sentences

_____

_____

_____

_____

_____

_____

_____

_____

_____

_____

_____

_____

_____

_____

At Home: Create dictionary entries together. If you want, make up silly words and your own definitions. Example: The word *scritch* means "to scratch and itch."

Name _____

A. Fill in the blank spaces below to form words with long i sounds. Blanks can be either vowels or consonants.

1. f l ___ ___ ___ + t =

_____

2. t ___ + e = _____

3. f i ___ + d = _____

4. f ___ + y = _____

5. w i ___ + d = _____

6. c h i ___ + d = _____

7. m i ___ + d = _____

8. m ___ ___ ___ + t =

_____

9. s t r i ___ + e =

_____

10. r e w i ___ + d =

_____

B. Add a consonant to the word in the first column. Make sure that the same consonant works for the word in the second column.

CVC		CVCe
11. f i ___	⟶	f i ___ e
12. k i ___	⟶	k i ___ e
13. h i ___	⟶	h i ___ e
14. p i ___	⟶	p i ___ e
15. r i ___	⟶	r i ___ e
16. d i ___	⟶	d i ___ e

© Macmillan/McGraw-Hill

At Home: Find unfamiliar long *i* words in a newspaper or magazine and write them down with a missing vowel or consonant as you did in the activity above.

Name _____

Answer each question with a complete sentence.

1. What situation have you <u>chuckled</u> at this week?

_____

2. How would you take a <u>photograph</u> of your friend? _____

_____

3. What do you like to eat when you have a big <u>appetite</u>? _____

_____

4. What does a puppy need to stay <u>healthy</u>? _____

_____

5. When have you been <u>nervous</u>? _____

_____

6. What might you keep in an <u>envelope</u>? _____

_____

7. What kinds of things <u>crackle</u>? _____

_____

8. Which animals have <u>down</u>? _____

_____

9. In what situation might you form a <u>huddle</u>? _____

_____

10. Which park is closest to your <u>neighborhood</u>? _____

_____

Use the words in the box to complete the crossword puzzle.

addressing	echoes	content	fierce	fumbled
manage	resort	starry	trudged	challenge

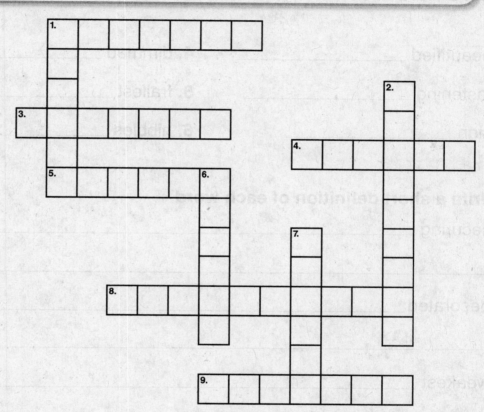

Across

1. dropped or handled in a clumsy way

3. walked slowly with heavy steps

4. be able to

5. repeats a sound

8. speaking to or handling a problem

9. happy and satisfied

Down

1. very strong

2. task that requires extra effort

6. full of stars

7. to seek help or go to for assistance

| securing | decorated | weakest | darkened | symbol | gnaws |

A. Match each vocabulary word from the box at the top of the page with a word it is related to below:

1. beautified _____

2. fastening _____

3. sign _____

4. dimmed _____

5. frailest _____

6. nibbles _____

B. Write a short definition of each word.

7. securing _____

_____

8. decorated _____

_____

9. weakest _____

_____

10. darkened _____

_____

11. symbol _____

_____

12. gnaws _____

_____

© Macmillan/McGraw-Hill

Think about a movie or TV show you enjoyed. Fill in the chart with details of the performance. Then write a summary.

A GREAT PERFORMANCE	
Title	_____
Type	_____
Characters' names	_____
When and where	_____ _____
Important events	_____ _____ _____ _____ _____
Opinion	_____

Summary: _____

_____

_____

_____

At Home: Ask your child to summarize a favorite story.

Name _____

As you read *The Strongest One*, fill in the Story Map.

Character

Setting

Beginning

Middle

End

How does the information you wrote in this Story Map help you generate questions about *The Strongest One*?

 At Home: Have your child use the chart to retell the story.

© Macmillan/McGraw-Hill

As I read, I will pay attention to punctuation.

	Dorje: My dear friend, I have come to ask a favor. I
12	need to travel to the city to visit my old uncle who is very
26	ill, and I need you to take care of an important matter for
39	me.
40	**Sonam:** You know I will always help an old friend.
50	**Dorje** *(holding out two bags)*: You see these two sacks
60	decorated with ancient symbols? Well, they are full of gold!
70	My father found this valuable treasure when he was a young
81	man. When he died, he left it to me. I am afraid to leave this
96	gold in my house when I am away. Will you please take care
109	of it for me?
113	**Sonam:** Oh, yes! Of course! I will keep your gold very
124	safe indeed.
126	**Narrator:** When Dorje heard this he was very glad. 135

Comprehension Check

1. What is Dorje's problem? **Problem and Solution**

2. In your own words, explain how Dorje solved his problem. **Summarize**

	Words Read	–	Number of Errors	=	Words Correct Score
First Read		–		=	
Second Read		–		=	

At Home: Help your child read the passage, paying attention to the goal at the top of the page.

Write captions for the photos below.

1. _____

_____

_____

3. _____

_____

_____

2. _____

_____

_____

4. _____

_____

_____

Write an article using the information from the photos and captions above.

_____

_____

_____

At Home: Look at some family photographs with your child.
Ask your child to make up captions for each one.

Name _____

A. Write the antonyms of the words below.

1. longest _____

2. old _____

3. slow _____

4. tall _____

5. mean _____

B. Use the pairs of antonyms above and write them in the same sentence. Underline the antonyms.

6. _____

_____

7. _____

_____

8. _____

_____

9. _____

_____

10. _____

_____

At Home: Give your child a list of words and have him or her write the antonym to each.

The Strongest One • **Book 3.1/Unit 2** ◇ **43**

Name _____

**A. Write as many words on the lines as you can that
follow each rule.**

Rule 1. All these one-syllable words begin with the letter _m_ or _l,_ and have a
long _e_ sound in the middle that is spelled _ea._

_____

_____

Rule 2. All these one-syllable words begin with the letter _f_ or _s_ and have a
long _e_ sound in the middle that is spelled _ee._

_____

_____

Rule 3. All these one-syllable words end with the letter _e_ and have a long _e_
sound at the end.

_____

_____

**B. See how many words with a long e sound you can create by using
only the letters in the word below.**

meantime

_____

_____

At Home: Ask your child to replace one of the beginning
consonants in Rule 1 with a new consonant, then make up
new words that follow the rule with the new consonant.

Name _____

Read the paragraph. On each blank line, write the word from the box that makes sense. Circle the words in each sentence that help you figure out which word to write.

passion	dangerous	splendid	ached
bothering	admire	concentrate	

Juan has a _____ for reading. He would rather read than

do anything else. Today, he's reading a _____ story about a
wolf named Pepper. The story is wonderful! Pepper is trying to find

his way home after a long journey. Juan wants to _____
because he's reading the best part of the story. Pepper has just walked into

a _____ part of the woods. Nearby, grizzly bears attack

small animals. Juan knows that Pepper's foot has _____ for
days, ever since Pepper stepped on a sharp rock. His foot has been

_____ him as he limps slowly along. At the end of the story,

Pepper makes it home safely. Juan tells his teacher, "I _____
the author of this book. She writes the best stories ever!"

Write two sentences about a story you like. Use at least one vocabulary word in each sentence. Circle any words that help the reader figure out the meaning of the vocabulary word.

_____

_____

_____

_____

Name _____

Write a story about two wolves and what they do during the day. One story should be a fantasy and one should be a reality. Be sure to use the same characters in each.

Fantasy

_____

_____

_____

_____

_____

_____

Reality

_____

_____

_____

_____

_____

_____

© Macmillan/McGraw-Hill

At Home: Have your child choose an object at home and tell how to write about it in two ways—fantasy and reality.

Name _____

As you read Wolf!, fill in the Fantasy and Reality Chart.

Fantasy	Reality

How does the information you wrote in the Fantasy and Reality Chart
help you generate questions about Wolf!?

At Home: Have your child use the chart to retell the story

Name _____

As I read, I will pay attention to punctuation and intonation.

	You see, I'm a lone wolf. I used to be in a wolf pack,
14	but they threw me out. Ever since then, I've been roaming
25	the forest and looking for a new group of friends.
35	Unfortunately, that's turned out to be more difficult
43	than I'd anticipated. Wolf packs prefer to keep outsiders
52	out. After a long, cold winter, I hadn't found a pack to
64	join, and I was very lonely.
70	Then I realized there might be another possibility. I
79	hadn't been hanging out with any other animals. From
88	what I saw as I went roaming, there were many different
99	kinds. So what if I hadn't found a pack of wolves? Maybe
111	I'd be happier in a gaggle of geese, a herd of elephants, a
124	pride of lions, or a school of fish.
132	I crossed through the forest, looking everywhere for
140	new friends. 142

Comprehension Check

1. Why is Wolf having a difficult time finding a new pack to join? **Plot**

2. What plan does Wolf come up with? **Problem and Solution**

	Words Read	−	Number of Errors	=	Words Correct Score
First Read		−		=	
Second Read		−		=	

© Macmillan/McGraw-Hill

At Home: Help your child read the passage, paying attention to the goal at the top of the page.

Name _____

Read the article about wolves and then answer the questions below.

Wolves

by Sean Ambrose

Just the Facts

There are three species or types of wolves: the gray wolf, *Canis lupus*, the red wolf, *Canis rufus*, and the Ethiopian wolf, *Canis simensis*. In 2004 there were close to 4,000 gray wolves in the wild. This is thanks to a huge recovery effort to bring wolves back from the edge of extinction.

A wolf can live up to 11 years but typically does not live past eight years old. The average wolf is less than five feet long and usually weighs less than a hundred pounds. Even though they are known as "gray" wolves, their fur can also be black or white.

People Predators

Wolves try to avoid people; however, people pose the biggest threat. The main threat to their survival is the loss of their habitat or home. The gray wolf has been on the endangered species list for a long time but is close to coming off. By learning more about wolves, people will have a better chance of seeing them in the future.

1. Identify a heading. _____

2. Identify an example of boldface type.

   _____

3. Identify an example of italics.

   _____

   _____

4. Use a dictionary to look up the pronunciation of *predators, endangered,* and *extinction.*

   _____

© Macmillan/McGraw-Hill

At Home: Have your child locate reading material at home to show you examples of each of the following: heading, boldface type, italics, pronunciation.

Wolf! • **Book 3.1/Unit 2** 49

Name _____

**Use a dictionary to find meanings for the words listed
below. Then, write a sentence that includes each word
twice, using two different meanings. Circle words that give
clues for each meaning.**

Example: horn Dave stopped (playing) his **horn** when he heard Mom
honk the (car's) **horn.**

1. catch _____

_____

2. force _____

_____

3. master _____

_____

4. just _____

_____

5. panel _____

_____

6. general _____

_____

7. chest _____

_____

At Home: Ask your child to write a sentence about the
school day that includes a multiple-meaning word two times.
Have your child explain the clues to each meaning.

Answer each riddle with a word that has *ch* or *tch*.

1. If something costs fifty cents and you pay with a dollar, you get me back.
What am I? _____

2. I am what you do before you exercise so you don't hurt yourself. What
am I? _____

3. If you miss me in the middle of your day, you may get very hungry. What
am I? _____

4. If you could look down and see the bottom of your face, you'd see me.
What am I? _____

5. I can be anywhere on your body and you scratch to get rid of me. What
am I? _____

6. Come look for us if you want to play a game. We fit on a board. What
are we? _____

7. Take time to answer this one. You wear me on your wrist. What am I?

_____

Write one riddle of your own that has a one-word answer.
Be sure your answer is a word that contains *ch* or *tch*.
Exchange papers with a partner and answer each other's riddle.

8. _____

_____

At Home: Have your child ask you a riddle with a one-word
answer that has *ch* or *tch*. Ask for hints if you need them.

Wolf! • Book 3.1/Unit 2 ◇51◇

Read each set of words. Choose the vocabulary word that best describes the words in each group. Write the vocabulary word on the line.

> predictions   objects   computers   entertainment

1. dishes
   clothes
   appliances
   cars

   _____

3. the weather
   the future
   the winner
   the outcome

   _____

2. games
   CDs
   movies
   sports

   _____

4. PC
   laptop
   mainframe
   hand held

   _____

Use each vocabulary word in a sentence.

5. _____

   _____

6. _____

   _____

7. _____

   _____

8. _____

   _____

© Macmillan/McGraw-Hill

Read the paragraphs below. List the facts and opinions in the paragraphs. Remember that a *fact* can be proven to be true. An *opinion* is a belief that may not be supported by facts.

Because of advances in medical science, people will live longer. More people will probably want to grow their food in their own gardens. Scientists are now working on new forms of pest control. It looks as if pests will disappear for good.

The future will bring changes in transportation, too. New technology will improve gas mileage. But, everyone won't want to drive. Many people will want to get more exercise and will choose to ride bicycles.

1. _____

_____

2. _____

_____

3. _____

_____

4. _____

_____

5. _____

_____

At Home: Read a newspaper with your child and determine
if specific information in the newspaper is fact or opinion.

What's in Store for the Future? **53**
Book 3.1/Unit 2

As you read *What's in Store for the Future?*, fill in the Fact and Opinion Chart.

Fact	Opinion

How does the information you wrote in the Fact and Opinion Chart help you summarize *What's in Store for the Future?*

At Home: Have your child use the chart to retell the story.

© Macmillan/McGraw-Hill

As I read, I will pay attention to my pronunciation of vocabulary words and other difficult words.

	Many people believe when there is a need, someone
9	comes up with an idea to meet that need. This is certainly
21	true for many inventions that have changed the way we
31	travel.
32	Long ago the only way to travel on land was by foot.
44	People could go only as far or as fast as their legs would
57	take them. As time went on, people wanted to move farther
68	and faster. They wanted to carry goods from one place to
79	another. They had to find ways to do this.
88	About 5,500 years ago, someone realized that round
95	**objects,** such as logs, could roll. This led to the important
106	invention of the wheel. If you placed a log under an **object,**
118	you could push it more easily. The wheel opened new doors
129	for people. It led to new vehicles. 136

Comprehension Check

1. What makes people invent things? **Make Inferences**

2. Why was the invention of the wheel important? **Main Idea and Details**

	Words Read	–	Number of Errors	=	Words Correct Score
First Read		–		=	
Second Read		–		=	

© Macmillan/McGraw-Hill

At Home: Help your child read the passage, paying attention to the goal at the top of the page.

What's in Store for the Future? 55
Book 3.1/Unit 2

Name _____

**Suppose you are writing a book on what the future will
be like. Using the blank pages below, fill in the different parts
of your book.**

At Home: Together with your child, look through two
fiction and two nonfiction books. Have your child point out
differences in the parts of each book.

Name _____

Add -s or -es to make each word plural.

1. hoax _____

2. chief _____

3. couch _____

4. catch _____

5. piano _____

6. daisy _____

7. ditch _____

8. bus _____

9. friend _____

10. pony _____

Write a short paragraph about what future schools will be like. Use at least five words in their plural form. Each plural should end in *-s* or *-es*.

_____

_____

_____

_____

_____

_____

_____

_____

_____

_____

At Home: Ask your child to find four or five objects in your home that form the plural by adding *-es.*

Name _____

**A. The letters *th, wh, ph* and *sh* can be found at the beginning,
   in the middle, or at the end of many words. Use a word
   with one of these patterns to complete each sentence.**

1. The opposite of thin is _____.

2. If it is a sunny day, you can usually look down and see your

   _____.

3. After winning the final game, the team won a _____.

4. If you want to know about something, you might begin your question

   with the word _____.

B. Write six sentences using words that have *th, ph, wh,* or *sh*.

5. _____

6. _____

7. _____

8. _____

9. _____

10. _____

At Home: Take turns telling riddles in which the answer is a
word with *th, ph, wh,* or *sh*. Say, for example, "You might use
me to remove snow" (shovel).

© Macmillan/McGraw-Hill

A. Think about the meaning of each vocabulary word. Then write a sentence containing the word. Make sure your sentence shows that you know the definition of the vocabulary word.

1. solar system _____

_____

2. dim _____

_____

3. easily _____

_____

4. temperatures _____

_____

5. farther _____

_____

6. telescope _____

_____

7. main _____

_____

8. probably _____

_____

**Read the two summaries below. Then write a paragraph that
the summary could be about.**

1. Summary: Dara's friends invited her to go to the movies, but she stayed
   home and finished her planet project instead.

   a. My paragraph _____

   _____

   _____

   _____

   _____

   _____

2. Summary: At the observatory, Esteban saw the Big Dipper and other
   constellations through a telescope.

   a. My paragraph _____

   _____

   _____

   _____

   _____

   _____

At Home: Ask your child to summarize a favorite story or
article. Ask your child how he or she decided which details to
include in a summary.

Name _____

As you read *The Planets in Our Solar System*, fill in the Main Idea Chart.

Main Idea	Details

How does the information you wrote in the Main Idea Chart help you generate questions about *The Planets in Our Solar System*?

 At Home: Have your child use the chart to retell the story.

As I read, I will pay attention to my pronunciation of vocabulary words.

7	On October 4, 1957, the world changed forever. That day, the Soviet Union launched the first satellite into space.
17	It was called Sputnik I. It was a small metal ball that
28	sent radio signals back to Earth. It orbited Earth at
38	18,000 miles (28,968.19 km) per hour, more than ten times
45	faster than any vehicle before it.
51	The success of Sputnik I proved that a machine could
60	survive in space. Could a person survive in space too?
70	**Probably**. But no one knew.
75	The Soviet Union tried to find out. They took the first
86	step by sending a dog into space. When Sputnik 2 blasted
96	off, Laika, the dog, was the first creature to travel in space.
108	Scientists measured Laika's breathing, heart rate, and
115	body **temperature**. Since the dog stayed healthy, they felt
124	it would be safe to send a person into space. 134

Comprehension Check

1. What lesson was learned with the success of Sputnik 1? **Main Idea and Details**

2. In your own words, explain why the Soviet Union sent a dog into space. **Summarize**

	Words Read	−	Number of Errors	=	Words Correct Score
First Read		−		=	
Second Read		−		=	

© Macmillan/McGraw-Hill

At Home: Help your child read the passage, paying attention to the goal at the top of the page.

Name _____

Answer these questions about the Internet.

1. When would an Internet article probably be more helpful than an article in a magazine? Why?

_____

_____

_____

2. How could the Internet help with your school work?

_____

_____

_____

3. Compare the Internet and the library in helping you write a report. Which do you like better?

_____

_____

_____

4. Besides school work, what else could the Internet help with?

_____

_____

_____

At Home: Open a magazine or newspaper and ask your child which are good articles for the Internet and why. Suggest that including several pictures is one reason why.

Use the sentence model below as you write a paragraph that includes words with their definitions. Your paragraph may be fiction or nonfiction, but it should relate to space travel or the planets in our solar system. Use the words below in your paragraph and define them. Circle each word you have defined and underline its definition.

He thought he would never get over the *disappointment,* an event that failed to be what he had expected.

horizon	descend	demonstrate
marvel	equipment	laboratory

_____

_____

_____

_____

_____

_____

_____

_____

© Macmillan/McGraw-Hill

At Home: Ask your child to explain how definitions within a text can help a reader understand a story or article. Invite your child to show you an example.

A. Look at the example of the tongue twister below using 4 words with a consonant blend. Write a tongue twister of your own in the spaces provided using 4 words for the *str*, *scr*, *spr*, and *thr* blends. Try to write each tongue twister about space or planets.

Example: The strong string stretches the strap.

1. str: _____

_____

2. scr: _____

_____

3. spr: _____

_____

4. thr: _____

B. Write one sentence using a *str*, *scr*, *spr*, and *thr* word in it.

5. _____

_____

_____

At Home: Ask your child to use the words *threw, three, thrill,* and *thread* to make up a tongue twister to tell you. Repeat the tongue twister three times quickly.

The Planets in Our Solar System
Book 3.1/Unit 2   65

© Macmillan/McGraw-Hill

Name _____

Write a sentence using the vocabulary word and underline the word in the sentence.

1. proper _____

_____

_____

2. talented _____

_____

_____

3. useful _____

_____

_____

4. single _____

_____

_____

5. excitement _____

_____

_____

6. acceptance _____

_____

_____

Write two or three sentences to inform, to entertain, and to persuade readers about their favorite hobby.

inform _____

_____

_____

_____

entertain _____

_____

_____

_____

_____

_____

persuade _____

_____

_____

Which is your favorite purpose for writing and why? _____

_____

_____

© Macmillan/McGraw-Hill

At Home: Talk with your child about familiar TV shows. Ask your child if the show is meant to entertain, to inform, or to persuade.

Author: A True Story • **Book 3.1/Unit 2** ◆ 67

Name _____

As you read *Author: A True Story*, fill in the Author's Purpose Chart.

Clues

↓

Author's Purpose

How does the information you wrote in the Author's Purpose Chart help you summarize *Author: A True Story*?

 At Home: Have your child use the chart to retell the story.

As I read, I will pay attention to sentence length.

	Some time around 1773, a Cherokee woman named
7	Wuh-teh gave birth to a son named Sequoyah. No one
17	knows the exact date of his birth, because the Cherokee
27	did not keep written records.
32	Wuh-teh lived with her son in Taskigi, in the Smoky
42	Mountains of Tennessee. Sequoyah's father was a fur
50	trader from Virginia who left Wuh-Teh to raise her son alone.
61	Young Sequoyah walked with a limp, but no one knows
71	for sure how he got it.
77	A Cherokee boy hunted and fished with the men of his
88	village. He played games that involved running,
95	throwing, and shooting with a bow and arrow. Sequoyah
104	knew he could never be the fastest runner or the best hunter.
116	Still, he must have longed for some way to gain acceptance
127	from his friends. 130

Comprehension Check

1. Why isn't the exact date of Sequoyah's birth known? **Main Idea and Details**

2. What do you think was important to young Cherokee boys? **Draw Conclusions**

	Words Read	–	Number of Errors	=	Words Correct Score
First Read		–		=	
Second Read		–		=	

At Home: Help your child read the passage, paying attention to the goal at the top of the page.

Author: A True Story • Book 3.I/Unit 2 ◇69◇

Name _____

**Write a poem about your favorite after-school activity.
Repeat at least one line. Include two or more examples of
alliteration. Remember that a poem does not have to rhyme.
Underline the repeated lines, and circle the alliterated sounds.**

_____

_____

_____

_____

_____

_____

_____

_____

_____

_____

_____

_____

_____

_____

_____

_____

© Macmillan/McGraw-Hill

At Home: Have your child find a few favorite poems or
rhymes. Then have your child point out any examples of
repetition and alliteration in the poems or rhymes.

Read each sentence and look at the underlined word. Write the correct meaning of the word. Then write a new sentence that includes the underlined word.

1. I found the <u>biography</u> on the author very interesting. The book had information about her entire life.

Meaning: _____

Sentence: _____

_____

2. Mrs. Phillips told us a <u>folk tale</u> in class today. It was a story her parents were told when they were little, and that they told Mrs. Phillips when she was a little girl.

Meaning: _____

Sentence: _____

_____

3. My mother found a <u>paperback</u> on the bus. The paper cover was very worn and folded, but all the pages were perfect.

Meaning: _____

Sentence: _____

_____

4. The article in the newspaper was so <u>humorous</u>. We all laughed at how funny it was.

Meaning: _____

Sentence: _____

_____

At Home: Have your child make up context clues for made-up words for you to figure out.

© Macmillan/McGraw-Hill

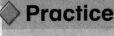
Name _____

Imagine that you have gone on vacation. Write a journal entry using at least eight of the words listed below to describe something that happens. Share your journal entry with a partner.

wrap	knit	sign	write	wrong
knight	wreck	wrists	knots	wring
wrote	gnat	knock	gnaws	know

_____

_____

_____

_____

_____

_____

_____

_____

_____

_____

_____

_____

 At Home: Play a game of word scramble, using only words with *gn, kn,* or *wr.* For example, unscramble *ornwg* to spell *wrong.*

Name _____

Write a sentence with each of the words listed below.

1. telescope: _____

_____

2. computers: _____

_____

3. dim: _____

_____

4. farther: _____

_____

5. dangerous: _____

_____

6. securing: _____

_____

7. predictions: _____

_____

8. darkened: _____

_____

9. splendid: _____

_____

10. solar system: _____

_____

Name _____

Write the definition of the word, then write a sentence correctly using the word.

1. ached _____

   _____

   _____

2. admire _____

   _____

   _____

3. symbol _____

   _____

   _____

4. objects _____

   _____

   _____

5. single _____

   _____

   _____

6. gnaws _____

   _____

   _____

Name _____

| gaze | agreeable | guests |
| banquet | untrusting | curiosity |

Fill in the blanks in the poem with the correct words from the box.

An Ode to Raw Fish and Seaweed

Raw fish wrapped in rice and green seaweed

You might say it's disgusting,

but I'm not that _____.

It's my belief and favorite hobby

to sample this unusual _____.

Mmmm—the taste, so unbelievable!

But so pleasantly likeable and _____.

I dream of a summer picnic blanket

spread under a raw sushi _____.

At the colorful fish rolls, I fix my _____.

Bright pink wrapped in dark green, I'm so amazed.

If my friends and _____ passed on the fish I like best,

I'll be sure to eat all the rest!

A. A group of people went to a new restaurant. Based on what each person said, make inferences about what he or she thought of the restaurant and food.

1. "I think we should leave the waiter a big tip," said Mom. _____

_____

2. "Next time I'm going to bring earplugs," said Dad. _____

_____

3. "At these prices we can eat here again tomorrow night," said Jim.

_____

4. "I love what they have done with the interior of this place," said Mom.

_____

_____

5. "Next time we should come earlier and get a better parking spot," said

Dad. _____

_____

B. Think of a time you went to a new restaurant or ate a food that was new to you. Write down something you said. Then write an inference another person might make based on your words.

6. _____

_____

_____

_____

At Home: Tell your child something about your day. Have your child make an inference based on your description.

As you read *Stone Soup*, fill in the Inference Map.

Clue	→	Clue	→	Clue	→	Inference

Clue	→	Clue	→	Clue	→	Inference

How does the information you wrote in this Inference Map help you visualize details in *Stone Soup*?

© Macmillan/McGraw-Hill

At Home: Have your child use the chart to retell the story.

As I read, I will pay attention to punctuation.

	Dan pulled his shopping list out of his pocket. He had a
12	long list of errands he had to run in the village shops.
24	He bought two pounds of whole-wheat flour from the
34	baker and a block of goat cheese from the cheese maker.
45	He bought red and green apples from the farmer and a
56	cake of bath soap from the soap maker. He bought
66	cinnamon and nutmeg from the spice merchant and a
75	length of cotton cloth from the weaver. One by one he
86	placed all of the goods he bought into a basket for the long
99	trip back up the hill.
104	When he had everything he needed, he set out for
114	home, but he didn't get very far. The heat from the late
126	afternoon sun made Dan feel hot and tired. 134

Comprehension Check

1. What does the word "errands" mean? **Main Idea and Details**

2. How did the heat affect Dan's walk home? **Summarize**

	Words Read	–	Number of Errors	=	Words Correct Score
First Read		–		=	
Second Read		–		=	

© Macmillan/McGraw-Hill

At Home: Help your child read the passage, paying attention to the goal at the top of the page.

Name _____

Complete the two charts below. On the first chart, write the column headings and your favorite foods, drinks, and places to eat. Fill in the second chart with the column headings and your least favorite of the same things. Remember that places to eat might include people's homes and parks as well as restaurants.

FAVORITES		
Foods		

LEAST FAVORITES		

At Home: Ask your child to think of a new category to add to both charts. Then have your child fill in that section on each chart.

◆ **Practice**

Vocabulary Strategy:
Synonyms

Name _____

**Rewrite each sentence, replacing each underlined word
with a synonym from the box.**

disaster	wonderful	consumed	chef
popped	stop	disagree	avoid
pile	dish	home	exciting

1. I did not want to <u>argue</u> with the waiter, but I could not <u>escape</u> it.

   _____

   _____

2. You cannot <u>prevent</u> the <u>cook</u> from making the dish he chooses to make.

   _____

   _____

3. There was still a <u>heap</u> of potatoes left on the <u>plate</u>.

   _____

   _____

4. We all went to my <u>house</u> after the <u>catastrophe</u> of a meal we had at the
   new restaurant.

   _____

   _____

5. At the end of the <u>delightful</u> party, we <u>burst</u> the balloons that were
   hanging around the restaurant.

   _____

   _____

© Macmillan/McGraw-Hill

At Home: Ask your child to think of two or three different
synonyms for a few of the words in the box.

In two minutes list as many one-syllable words as you can that
have the /är/ sound as in *harm* and the /ôr/ sound as in *port*.
Then write four sentences, each using two words from your lists.
Underline the <u>ar</u> and <u>or</u> words you use.

ar as in *harm*	or as in *port*
_____	_____
_____	_____
_____	_____
_____	_____
_____	_____

1. _____

_____

2. _____

_____

3. _____

_____

4. _____

_____

At Home: Ask your child to find words in newspapers or
magazines that have the same vowel sound as *harm* or *port*.

wearily	depart	suitable	increase
observed	advised	discouraged	

**Write a sentence using each vocabulary word from the box.
Underline the vocabulary word.**

1. _____

_____

2. _____

_____

3. _____

_____

4. _____

_____

5. _____

_____

6. _____

_____

7. _____

_____

Choose one plot and one setting from the lists below. Use both to write a story.

Plots

- A person must overcome his or her fear of water to save a friend.

- A ten-year-old must find an old letter to solve a mystery.

- A photographer working on a newspaper story loses his or her camera.

- A person or animal must answer a riddle correctly to help someone.

Settings

- a pioneer town in the 1800s

- the mountains in the present time

- a beach in the distant future

- a supermarket in the present time

- a planet in the past, present, or future

_____

_____

_____

_____

_____

_____

_____

_____

_____

At Home: Together make up stories with unusual plots and settings. Try different kinds of stories, such as a humorous story, a mystery, and science fiction.

One Riddle, One Answer
Book 3.1/Unit 3

83

Name _____

As you read One Riddle, One Answer, fill in the Setting Web.

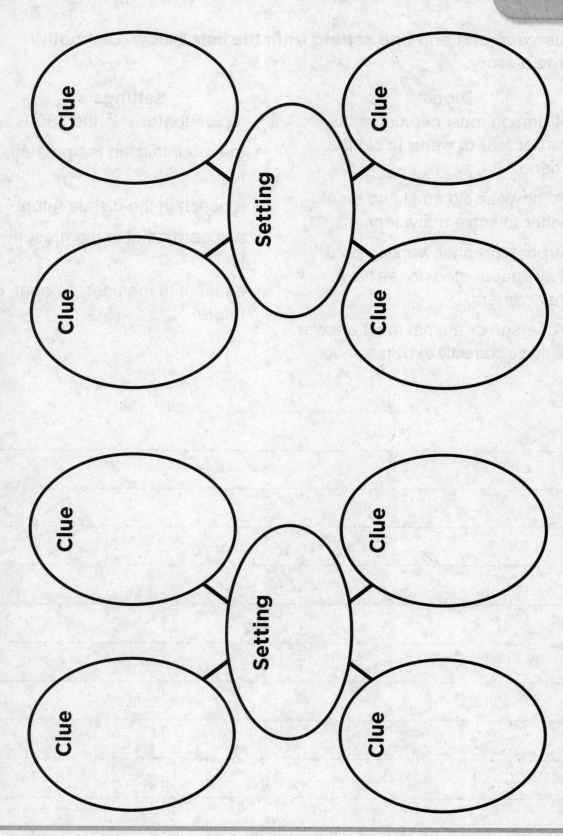

How does the information you wrote in this Setting Web help you analyze story structure in *One Riddle, One Answer?*

At Home: Have your child use the chart to retell the story.

Name _____

As I read, I will pay attention to pauses and intonation.

	"Are you ready for a math contest?" Kara asked.
9	"It's time to ride Pixie," Kevin reminded her. " We'll
18	have a contest later."
22	Kara said, "I'll write an equation in the dirt. Whoever
32	answers it gets to ride Pixie for the entire hour."
42	"You might pick an equation you already know," Kevin
51	pointed out.
53	"You pick the first number of the equation and I'll
63	finish it," Kara suggested.
67	That seemed suitable to Kevin. Kara was younger and knew
77	less math. It would be great to ride Pixie for the entire
89	hour. "Okay, I pick the number six," he agreed.
98	Kara found a stick and wrote the number six in the dirt.
110	"Now, I'll pick a number," she said. "I pick the number
121	seven." She wrote in the dirt: 6+7=?
127	"What's the answer to that?" she asked.
134	Kevin was surprised. How did she know the one
143	equation he wouldn't be able to solve? 150

Comprehension Check

1. Why did Kevin think he would win the contest? **Make Inferences**

2. What surprises Kevin? **Plot**

	Words Read	−	Number of Errors	=	Words Correct Score
First Read		−		=	
Second Read		−		=	

At Home: Help your child read the passage, paying attention to the goal at the top of the page.

Name _____

**Write two riddles. Include consonance in the first. Include at least
one metaphor in the second. Draw a picture for each riddle.**

Riddle 1— Consonance

_____

_____

_____

Riddle 2— Metaphor

_____

_____

_____

At Home: Together, look for examples of consonance and
metaphor in magazine advertisements.

© Macmillan/McGraw-Hill

Choose the word from the box that best completes the sentence.
Write the definition and create your own sentence.

apply	fade	crumpled	mound	stern

1. I had to _____ a lot of tape so the poster did not fall.

_____

_____

2. We had to be _____ with my cat because it kept running out the door.

_____

_____

3. My stack of papers _____ when my dog ran into the table.

_____

_____

4. There is a _____ of dirt at the park that my brother and I love to play on.

_____

_____

5. The color on the cover of my book began to _____ after I had it for a long time.

_____

_____

At Home: Ask your child to read a newspaper and write down any unfamiliar words. Then have him or her look them up.

Name _____

List as many words as you can that have the letters *are*, *air*, and *ear* that stand for the vowel sound in *dare*, *fair*, and *bear*. Then, write two riddles. Make the answer to each riddle a word from your list.

are as in *dare*	*air* as in *fair*	*ear* as in *bear*

Riddles

_____

_____

_____

_____

_____

_____

_____

_____

_____

 At Home: Have your child ask you three riddles with one-word answers that each has the vowel sound in *dare*, *fair*, and *bear*.

Brainstorm some ideas that would benefit both the animals and the people in your community. Then write a speech that you would give to the people of your community, asking them to assist you. Use each of the vocabulary words at least once. Underline the words.

preserve	suffered	restore	rainfall

_____

_____

_____

_____

_____

_____

_____

_____

_____

_____

_____

> The **cause** is what makes something happen.
>
> The **effect** is what happens.

**Write a sentence for each missing cause or effect that
makes sense.**

1. Cause: Trash was thrown into the ocean.

   Effect: _____

   _____

2. Cause: _____

   _____

   Effect: The balloon popped.

3. Cause: Water flowed steadily across rocks for many years.

   Effect: _____

   _____

4. Cause: _____

   _____

   Effect: The tomato plants grew well.

5. Cause: Fires burned down several acres of the state forest.

   Effect: _____

   _____

© Macmillan/McGraw-Hill

At Home: Have your child tell you possible effects of a
weather condition, such as rain, hot sun, a hurricane,
or a tornado, on a person or town.

**As you read *Saving the Sand Dunes*, fill in the
Cause and Effect Chart.**

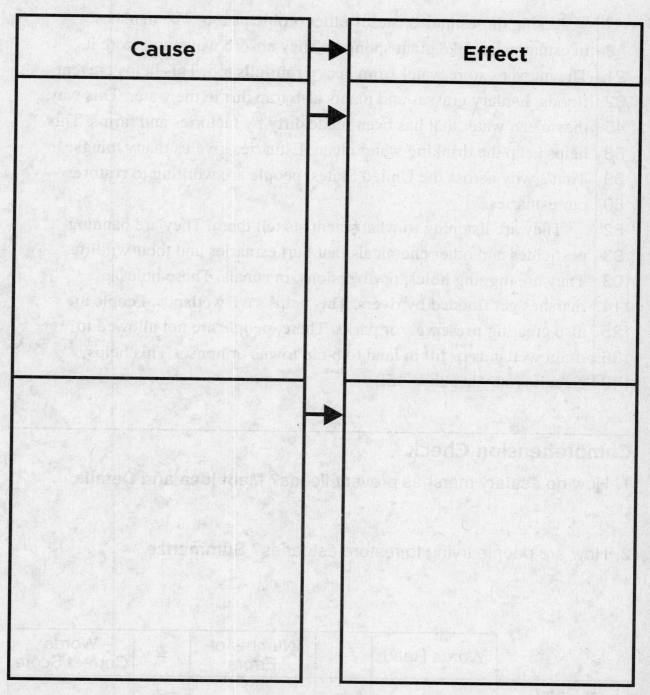

Cause		Effect
	→	
	→	
	→	

**How does the information you wrote in this Cause and Effect Chart help
you analyze text structure in *Saving the Sand Dunes*?**

At Home: Have your child use the chart to retell the story.

As I read, I will pay attention to my pronunciation of vocabulary words and other difficult words.

	Losing our estuaries causes other problems too. The marshes
9	in estuaries are like giant sponges. They absorb water and store it.
21	The marshes store water from heavy **rainfalls** too. This helps prevent
32	floods. Estuary grasses and plants also trap dirt in the water. This way,
45	they clean water that has been made dirty by factories and farms. This
58	helps keep the drinking water clean. Estuaries give us many things.
69	That's why across the United States, people are working to **restore**
80	our estuaries.
82	They are listening to what scientists tell them. They are banning
93	pesticides and other chemicals that hurt estuaries and their wildlife.
103	They are digging holes, or diversions, in canals. These holes let
114	marshes get flooded by rivers. This helps save wetlands. People are
125	also creating **preserves**, or parks. There, people are not allowed to
136	drain wetlands or fill in land to build towns or houses. This helps
149	estuaries stay healthy. 152

Comprehension Check

1. How do estuary marshes prevent floods? **Main Idea and Details**

2. How are people trying to restore estuaries? **Summarize**

	Words Read	−	Number of Errors	=	Words Correct Score
First Read		−		=	
Second Read		−		=	

© Macmillan/McGraw-Hill

At Home: Help your child read the passage, paying attention to the goal at the top of the page.

Name _____

You have been assigned to research and write a newspaper article about pollution in a nearby lake. Listed below are different library resources. Next to each one, write what you do with it to research your topic. You do not have to write the article.

1. Electronic card catalog: _____

_____

_____

_____

2. Newspapers and periodicals: _____

_____

_____

_____

3. Telephone directory: _____

_____

_____

_____

4. Which library resource would you use first and why?

_____

_____

_____

© Macmillan/McGraw-Hill

At Home: Ask your child to explain why a newspaper might have information that a book does not. Ask your child to tell you which library resources he or she has used most.

Saving the Sand Dunes
Book 3.1/Unit 3

93

**Look up each multiple-meaning word in the dictionary. Choose
two different definitions of the word and write each definition
under the word. Write a riddle for each definition of the word.**

Example:

line
Riddle 1: <u>I rhyme with mine. You stand in me when you wait for your</u>
<u>turn. What am I?</u>
Riddle 2: <u>I rhyme with mine. If you have a big part in a play, you have</u>
<u>to learn many more than one of me. What am I?</u>

1. block
   Definition 1: _____

   Definition 2: _____

   Riddle 1: _____

   _____

   Riddle 2: _____

   _____

2. raise
   Definition 1: _____

   Definition 2: _____

   Riddle 1: _____

   _____

   Riddle 2: _____

   _____

 At Home: Ask your child to tell you two meanings for the
word *note* and to explain how to tell which meaning is correct
in a sentence.

A. Write a sentence for the words with the /ûr/ sound below and include another word that rhymes with it that has a /ûr/ sound. The two words can have different spellings of the /ûr/ sound. Underline the two words.

Example: Terry was <u>first</u> in line because his <u>thirst</u> was the greatest.

1. bird _____

_____

2. earn _____

_____

3. turn _____

_____

4. girl _____

_____

5. purse _____

_____

6. serve _____

_____

B. Fill in the missing letters to complete each word with a /ûr/ sound.

7. l _____ n = _____

8. g _____ m = _____

9. f _____ m = _____

10. t _____ t l e = _____

At Home: Ask your child to tell you a sentence that uses two rhyming words that have different spellings for the /ûr/ sound (hearth, birth; bird, heard; turn, stern; curve, serve).

**Make up a story about a long car or bus trip. In your story
include at least one other character besides yourself. Use each
of the vocabulary words at least once and underline them.**

annual	potential	aisles	expensive
politely	innocent	package	wrapping

_____

_____

_____

_____

_____

_____

_____

_____

_____

_____

_____

_____

_____

_____

A. Read the paragraph below. Use clues in the paragraph to make an inference about what is happening and why.

> Matthew is the captain of the swim team. It is the night before the biggest meet of the year. When he starts packing his swim gear for the meet, Matthew suddenly needs to sit down on the end of his bed. He begins to feel dizzy.

Inference: _____

_____

_____

B. Write a paragraph that contains clues that will make the inference below make sense.
Inference: Nancy wants to enter the school writing contest.

_____

_____

_____

_____

_____

_____

_____

_____

_____

At Home: Ask your child to describe a situation when he or she needed to make an inference.

The Jones Family Express
Book 3.1/Unit 3
97

© Macmillan/McGraw-Hill

**As you read *The Jones Family Express*, fill in the
Inference Chart.**

Clues	Inference

How does the information you wrote in this Inference Chart help you
visualize details in *The Jones Family Express*?

At Home: Have your child use the chart to retell the story.

As I read, I will pay attention to punctuation and dialogue.

	Carl Simon was spending the last week before school
9	started with his Grandma Jackie. Her summer home on
18	Long Island was just two blocks from the Atlantic Ocean.
28	On the day that the amazing thing happened, they'd
37	spent all day together on the beach. Now, the sun was low
49	in the sky. Most people had already left the beach.
59	They stood at the edge of the water and watched
69	seabirds run along the shore. "They're looking for small
78	creatures that the waves wash in," Grandma told Carl.
87	She used American Sign Language to tell him this. Her
97	fingers moved quickly as she made the signs that stood for
108	letters and words.
111	Grandma Jackie had learned to sign when Carl was a
121	baby. That was when his family first realized that Carl
131	could not hear. He was deaf.
137	Carl was eight now and he had also learned American
147	Sign Language. He and his grandmother could talk
155	together easily. 157

Comprehension Check

1. What are the seabirds looking for? **Main Idea and Details**

2. How did Grandma Jackie communicate with Carl? **Summarize**

	Words Read	–	Number of Errors	=	Words Correct Score
First Read		–		=	
Second Read		–		=	

At Home: Help your child read the passage, paying attention to the goal at the top of the page.

Carlos is a new student at your school. You are trying to help him and his family. His mother needs to know how to drive from their house to the school. Read the information that follows. Then fill in the blank map to help Carlos's mother drive him to school. Label landmarks on the map that might help her.

Carlos lives on Maple Street. It is eight city blocks from the school. There are three stores, a park, and a firehouse on Carlos's way to school. There is also one right turn and one left turn. The school is on Walnut Street.

At Home: Ask your child to explain the directions, in a step-by-step order, for completing a household task, such as making the bed or raking the lawn.

© Macmillan/McGraw-Hill

Name _____

A. Use each pair of homophones in the same sentence.

1. weigh, way

_____

_____

2. herd, heard

_____

_____

3. ant, aunt

_____

_____

4. our, hour

_____

_____

5. bored, board

_____

_____

B. List several homophones of your own.

6. _____   _____

7. _____   _____

8. _____   _____

9. _____   _____

10. _____   _____

At Home: Use a pair of homophones in the same sentence.
Have your child say and spell each homophone.

The vowel diagraphs *oo* and *ue* stand for the /ü/ sound, as in *balloon* and *clue*. The vowel digraph *oo* also can stand for the /u̇/ sound, as in *good, cook,* or *wool.* In a word with the **CVCe** pattern, the letter *u* can stand for the /ū/ sound, as in *refuse* and *use.* The letters *ue* can also stand for the /ū/ as in *hue* or *cue,* or the /ü/ sound, as in *glue* or *true.*

Read the words aloud and decide if the sounds are alike or not. Write yes or no on the blank line.

1. Do *hood* and *food* have the same sound? _____

2. Do *fool* and *due* have the same sound? _____

3. Do *fuse* and *moon* have the same sound? _____

4. Do *fuel* and *huge* have the same sound? _____

5. Do *boot* and *look* have the same sound? _____

6. Do *cartoon* and *foot* have the same sound? _____

7. Do *Yule* and *fuel* have the same sound? _____

8. Do *mute* and *school* have the same sound? _____

9. Do *shook* and *mood* have the same sound? _____

10. Do *loose* and *roost* have the same sound? _____

At Home: Have your child tell you two sentences with rhyming words that have the vowel sound in *soon, book, true,* or *tune.*

Name _____

instance	illustrate	style
sketches	suggestions	textures

Write the vocabulary words in the crossword puzzle for the clues that are given. Write the clues below for the words given in the crossword puzzle.

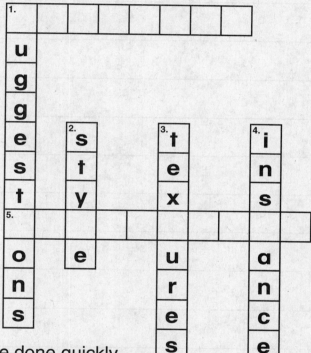

Across

1. drawings that are done quickly

5. to draw or add pictures

Down

1. _____

2. _____

3. _____

4. _____

Name _____

Write a paragraph describing in sequence the steps to making a painting. Use sequence words, such as *first, next, then,* and *finally,* to make the order of the steps sound clear. Underline the sequence words.

_____

_____

_____

_____

_____

_____

_____

_____

_____

_____

_____

_____

_____

_____

_____

_____

© Macmillan/McGraw-Hill

At Home: Ask your child to draw a picture and then describe the steps he or she followed to draw it.

As you read *What Do Illustrators Do?*, fill in the Sequence Chart.

Event

↓

Event

↓

Event

↓

Event

↓

Event

How does the information you wrote in this Inference Chart help you
analyze text structure in *What Do Illustrators Do?*

At Home: Have your child use the chart to retell the story.

What Do Illustrators Do?
Book 3.1/Unit 3
105

As I read, I will pay attention to tempo and punctuation.

	In fact, the artist is in control of a picture. Think about
12	photographing a scene. By adjusting the camera a little bit,
22	you can change what goes into your picture. Turn the
32	camera on its side and you will have a picture that is taller
45	than it is wide. Move the camera to one side and you will
58	make the composition, or plan, of the picture more
67	interesting. Drawing a landscape is similar to this.
75	One big choice you must make is where to put the
86	horizon. The horizon is the line where the earth meets the
97	sky. If the horizon is at the bottom of the picture, the picture
110	will seem very near. If it is close to the top, the picture will
124	seem far away.
127	There are no rules you have to follow when you draw
138	a landscape, but it is a good idea to think of your picture
151	as having three parts. Try to put something interesting in
161	each part. 163

Comprehension Check

1. What is a horizon? **Context Clues**

2. How can you give a picture more depth? **Summarize**

	Words Read	–	Number of Errors	=	Words Correct Score
First Read		–		=	
Second Read		–		=	

© Macmillan/McGraw-Hill

 At Home: Help your child read the passage, paying attention to the goal at the top of the page.

**Pretend you are a famous children's book illustrator.
A reporter asks you the following questions in an interview.
Write your answer to each interview question.**

Interviewer: When did you first realize you wanted to be a children's book illustrator?

1. You: _____

_____

Interviewer: What do you like to draw most? Why?

2. You: _____

_____

Interviewer: What are some of your favorite children's books? Why do you like them?

3. You: _____

_____

Interviewer: Do you think being a children's book illustrator is fun? Why or why not?

4. You: _____

_____

Interviewer: If you weren't an illustrator, what work would you want to do? Why?

5. You: _____

_____

At Home: Have your child interview you or other family members about their jobs. Have your child record the questions and responses on paper or with an audio recorder.

What Do Illustrators Do?
Book 3.1/Unit 3

107

**Write a sentence or two for each of the words below and
provide sentence clues for a reader to figure out the words.
Look up any unfamiliar words in a dictionary to help you. Try
to make all your sentences about illustrating or painting.**

Example: dawn: I woke up at dawn to make a painting of the sun
rising over the mountains.

1. landscapes: _____

_____

_____

2. blossoms: _____

_____

_____

3. improving: _____

_____

_____

4. exhibit: _____

_____

_____

5. endless: _____

_____

_____

At Home: Look through a magazine or newspaper with your
child. Have him or her use context clues to figure out any
unfamiliar words.

Name _____

A. Solve each riddle with a word that has the same vowel sound as the /oi/ sound in *boil* and *boy*.

1. I am a word you can use to describe a king or a queen.

   What am I? r __ __ al

2. I am what you make when you decide something.

   What am I? ch __ __ ce

3. I am on the tip of a sharp pencil.

   What am I? p __ __ nt

4. I am how you feel when something bothers you.

   What am I? ann __ __ ed

5. I am a meeting you have with a doctor.

   What am I? app __ __ ntment

6. I am a color that is a combination of blue and green.

   What am I? turqu __ __ se

B. Write two riddles for words with the same vowel sound as the /oi/ sound in *boil* and *boy*. Then write the answer to your riddle.

7. _____

   _____

8. _____

   _____

At Home: Ask your child to write a sentence that has at least three words that have the same vowel sound as the /oi/ sound in *boil* and *boy*.

Read these sentences and use the words below to fill in the blanks. The letters in the boxes spell a mystery word that will help you answer the question at the bottom of the page.

banquet	depart	discouraged	guests	preserve
rainfall	suffered	suitable	untrusting	wearily

1. She took an umbrella because she was so

___ ___ ___ ___ ___ ___ ___ [ ] ___ ___ of the weather.

2. Farmers love a huge ___ ___ ___ ___ ___ ___ [ ] ___ .

3. We ___ ___ ___ ___ ___ [ ] ___ packed up our heavy tools.

4. We decided to add special food and have a fancy

___ ___ ___ ___ [ ] ___ ___ at our house.

5. We couldn't use any food that had [ ] ___ ___ ___ ___ ___ ___ any water damage.

6. All the ___ ___ ___ ___ [ ] ___ were dressed up.

7. We hiked through the animal ___ [ ] ___ ___ ___ ___ ___ .

8. We had to ___ ___ ___ [ ] ___ ___ early because of the rain.

9. Some activities are not ___ ___ ___ [ ] ___ ___ ___ ___ for a baby.

10. I was not ___ ___ ___ ___ ___ ___ ___ ___ ___ [ ] ___ because I knew we would come back soon and see the animals.

11. What do you do when you draw pictures for a story?

• _____

12. Write the definition of the mystery word? _____

© Macmillan/McGraw-Hill

Name _____

Use the words from the box to complete the crossword puzzle.

curiosity	potential	style	restore
sketches	textures	wrapping	

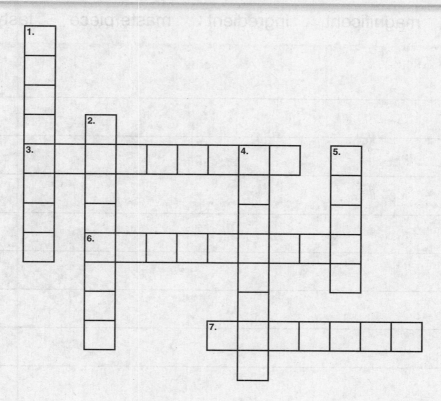

Across

3. something that is interesting because it is strange or unusual

6. capable of becoming something

7. to bring back to original condition

Down

1. simple drawings that are done quickly

2. something used to cover something

4. the way surfaces feel when you touch them

5. a particular way of doing something

Name _____

Write a paragraph about an animal that cooks or bakes a tasty dessert. You may choose a rooster, a pig, a duck, or another animal. Decide which dessert your animal will make. Use at least four of the words from the box in your paragraph.

| recipes | magnificent | ingredient | masterpiece | tasty |

_____

_____

_____

_____

_____

_____

_____

_____

_____

_____

_____

_____

Use the paragraphs below to answer the questions.

Some people call lemons the sunny fruit. The bright yellow color reminds them of the sun. Lemons have a thick skin that protects the juice and pulp inside. The zesty tart flavor of lemons is just perfect in cakes, candies, and drinks. Lemons ship well and are available throughout our country.

Peaches are an orange-pink color. They have a soft, fuzzy skin. The flesh of a ripe peach is soft, and the flavor is sweet. People often eat peaches out of their hands. They make a great snack. Peaches often turn up in pies in the summertime. Peaches bruise easily and must be shipped with care.

List four ways in which lemons and peaches differ.

1. _____

_____

2. _____

_____

3. _____

_____

4. _____

_____

5. What comparison about lemons, and peaches can you make based on these paragraphs?

_____

_____

At Home: Have your child compare and contrast two of his or her favorite snacks.

Cook-a Doodle-Doo!
Book 3.2/Unit 4
113

As you read *Cook-a-Doodle-Doo!*, fill in the Venn Diagram.

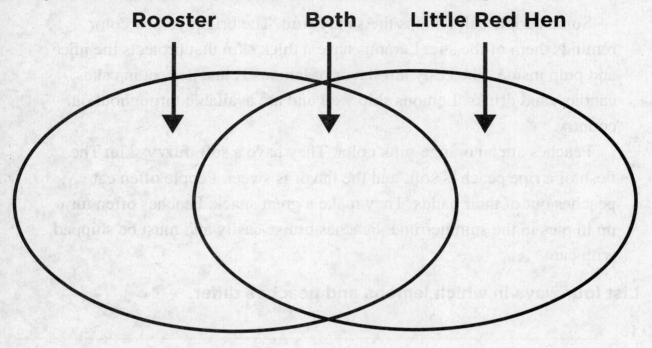

Rooster   Both   Little Red Hen

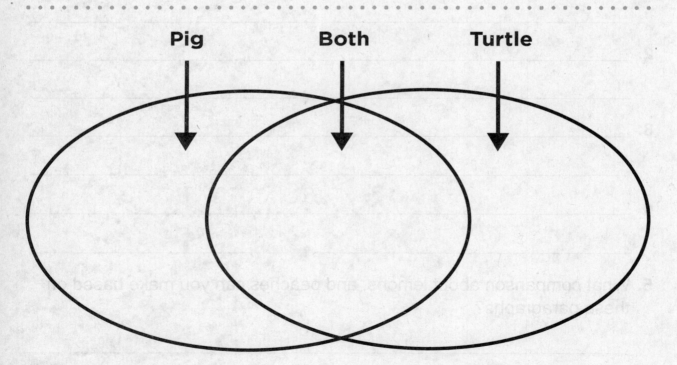

Pig   Both   Turtle

How does the information you wrote in this Venn Diagram help you
make inferences and analyze *Cook-a-Doodle-Doo!*?

 At Home: Have your child use the chart to retell the story.

As I read, I will pay attention to punctuation.

	People in ancient Greece and Rome ate seasoned flat
9	bread. It looked a little like the pizza crust we know
20	today. They added herbs, spices, and oil to make the bread
31	tasty. Egyptians made flat bread like this too. They made it
42	to celebrate the Pharaoh's birthday.
47	Scientists think Roman soldiers ate something like
54	pizza. They found traces of ovens where the men once
64	lived. The ovens were over 2,000 years old. They were
73	lined with stone. They looked like early pizza ovens!
82	In the 1600s, people who lived in Italy ate
90	simple round flat bread as their main food. They had little
101	to work with besides wheat flour, olive oil, and local
111	herbs. They called the bread "focaccia" (foh•KAH•chee•uh).
117	They were the first people to put tomatoes on their
127	flat bread. The first tomatoes brought to Italy were most
137	likely yellow. Italians called them "golden apples." 144

Comprehension Check

1. Why do scientists think Roman soldiers ate something similar to pizza?
Main Idea and Details

2. Why might we say that the people in Italy in the 1600s ate a dish
similar to our modern pizza? **Draw Conclusions**

	Words Read	−	Number of Errors	=	Words Correct Score
First Read		−		=	
Second Read		−		=	

At Home: Help your child read the passage, paying
attention to the goal at the top of the page.

**Think of how to make your favorite sandwich. Use the boxes
below to create a diagram showing how to make this sandwich.
Be sure to include a title and captions.**

1.

2.

3.

4.

5.

6.

At Home: Have your child choose one meal and explain
how to prepare it, including the ingredients required and the
steps in the preparation process.

Authors use *idioms* to make their language more colorful.
Write sentences using the idioms in the box.

> out to lunch
>
> between a rock and a hard place
>
> butter him up
>
> spill the beans
>
> sounds fishy

1. out to lunch: _____

_____

_____

2. spill the beans: _____

_____

_____

3. between a rock and a hard place: _____

_____

_____

4. sounds fishy: _____

_____

_____

5. butter him up: _____

_____

_____

At Home: Tell your child a food-related idiom (*can't cut the mustard; chew the fat; icing on the cake*). Ask your child to use the idiom in a sentence.

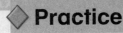
Name _____

Read the following paragraph and circle six words that have the /ô/ vowel sound. Then complete the story using at least three other words with the /ô/ vowel sound, spelled *aw* as in *drawing*, *al* as in *hall*, or *au* as in *maul*. Use a dictionary to check your work.

It was a beautiful autumn day. Paul walked to the store to buy a treat with his birthday money. He bought a large bag of popcorn. On the way home, Paul heard Maya call out, "Help!" He looked to his right and saw Maya lying on the ground.

Paul ran over to her to help. "Did you fall? What happened?" he asked.

"You will never believe what happened," she said as Paul helped her to her feet.

_____

_____

_____

_____

_____

_____

_____

_____

_____

_____

© Macmillan/McGraw-Hill

At Home: Tell your child a riddle in which the answer is a word with the /ô/ vowel sound. "You hold me by your fingers. You use me to write on some boards. What am I?" (chalk).

Use all the words below to write a fable about two animals that learn to get along with each other. Remember that all fables have a moral or teach a lesson.

argued	fabric	possessions
purchased	beamed	quarreling

_____

_____

_____

_____

_____

_____

_____

_____

_____

_____

_____

> To **draw conclusions,** pay attention to the facts and add
> information you already know from your own experiences.

**What conclusions can you draw from each paragraph below?
Write your conclusions on the lines that follow each paragraph.**

1. When he was President of the United States, Jimmy Carter helped
    Israel and Egypt reach a peace agreement. Later, he founded the Carter
    Center. The center helps people solve their disagreements. It also sends
    people to watch elections in different countries to make sure that they
    are fair. Carter and his wife also volunteer to build houses for people
    who could not afford them otherwise.

    _____

    _____

    _____

2. Mary Church Terrell worked to help women gain the right to vote. She
    was also a founder of the National Association of Colored Women.
    In Washington, D. C., she led a boycott against restaurants. She
    encouraged people not to eat at restaurants that refused to serve African
    Americans.

    _____

    _____

    _____

© Macmillan/McGraw-Hill

At Home: Talk about someone you know who has helped
others to get along. With your child, make a list of the
person's qualities or contributions.

As you read *Seven Spools of Thread*, fill in the Conclusion Map.

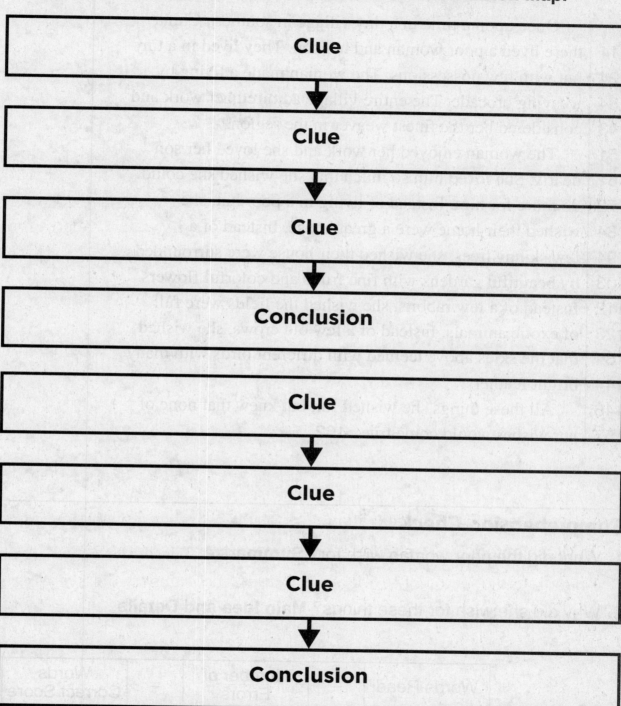

Clue

↓

Clue

↓

Clue

↓

Conclusion

Clue

↓

Clue

↓

Clue

↓

Conclusion

How does the information your wrote in this Conclusion Map help you make inferences and analyze *Seven Spools of Thread*?

 At Home: Have your child use the chart to retell the story.

As I read, I will pay attention to punctuation.

	Once upon a time in a tiny village in southern China
11	there lived a poor woman and her son. They lived in a tiny
24	hut with few possessions. The woman made a living by
34	weaving brocade. The entire village admired her work and
43	considered her the finest weaver in the region.
51	The woman enjoyed her work and she loved her son
61	dearly. She loved him so much that she wished she could
72	do more for him. Instead of living in a poor hut, she
84	wished their home were a great house. Instead of a
94	few skinny trees, she wished their house were surrounded
103	by beautiful gardens with fine fruits and colorful flowers.
112	Instead of a few rabbits, she wished the fields were full
123	of exotic animals. Instead of a few old crows, she wished
134	that the skies above teemed with different birds with many
144	bright feathers.
146	All these things she wished for, but knew that none of
157	her wishes would come true. 162

Comprehension Check

1. What did the poor woman wish for? **Summarize**

2. Why did she wish for these things? **Main Idea and Details**

	Words Read	−	Number of Errors	=	Words Correct Score
First Read		−		=	
Second Read		−		=	

 At Home: Help your child read the passage, paying attention to the goal at the top of the page.

Name _____

Create a list of rules for a club you are organizing. The rules should promote club members to get along and not to quarrel. Put a title on the top of your list of rules that includes your club's name.

_____

_____

1. _____

_____

2. _____

_____

3. _____

_____

4. _____

_____

5. _____

_____

6. _____

_____

_____

At Home: Together, write rules for doing chores or sharing things in your home.

Multiple-meaning words have more than one meaning. For example, the word *beamed* could mean "shone." The moon *beamed* down. *Beamed* could also mean "smiled." My coach *beamed* when we won the soccer match. Dictionaries give all the meanings of a word. The dictionary entry also shows the way a word is used in a sentence.

A. Use a dictionary to figure out the definition of each word in boldface type below. Write the correct definition for the way the word is used in the sentence. Then answer the question.

1. Can a baby **call?** _____

2. Can a flag **wave?** _____

3. Can a person catch a **cold?** _____

4. Can a **well** learn a lesson? _____

_____

5. Can you rub fabric between your **palms?** _____

_____

B. Write two different meanings for the word *rose.*

6. _____

_____

7. _____

_____

 At Home: Ask your child for different meanings of the words *excuse* and *punch.*

A. Choose the correct word from the box to answer each riddle. Make sure each word has the /ou/ sound, as in _found_ or _crowd_.

bounce	crouch	found	couch	allowed	round
louder	owl	plow	ground	proud	

1. A farmer may use me before planting. What am I? _____

2. Voices may become this way when people quarrel. What am I?

_____

3. I am a bird that you hear only at night. What am I?

_____

4. People like to sit on me and read or watch television. What am I?

_____

5. I am the shape of a circle. What am I? _____

B. Write your own riddle. Use another word from the box for your answer. Make sure the word has the /ou/ sound.

6. _____

_____

_____

At Home: Together, create silly poems that have the /ou/ sound.

Seven Spools of Thread
Book 3.2/Unit 4
125

Name _____

A. Write a sentence using each vocabulary word. Try to make each sentence about helping the environment.

1. native _____

_____

2. research _____

_____

3. shouldn't _____

_____

_____

4. sprout _____

_____

5. clumps _____

_____

B. Fill in the webs below with as many synonyms as you can for each word.

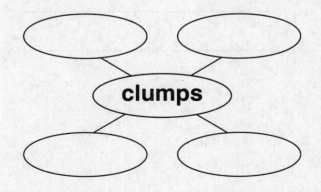

**Read the paragraph. Then compare and contrast the
different rain forests.**

Two Different Forests

Rain forests are filled with trees and plants. They are home to millions of animals. There are two main types of rain forests: temperate and tropical. Some tropical rain forests are near the equator. They are in South America, Africa, and Australia. Some temperate rain forests are along the west coast of the United States and Canada. There are more trees in tropical rain forests than in temperate ones. Both get over 80 inches of rain a year. However, in tropical rain forests it is almost always raining. Temperate rain forests have wet and dry seasons. The soil of a tropical rain forest is very old. Temperate rain forests have soil that has more nutrients in it.

Characteristics of a temperate rain forest:

_____

_____

_____

Characteristics of a tropical rain forest:

_____

_____

_____

Characteristics they share:

_____

_____

_____

At Home: Ask your child to compare living in
a rainforest with living in your neighborhood.

Washington Weed Whackers **127**
Book 3.2/Unit 4

© Macmillan/McGraw-Hill

Name _____

As you read *Washington Weed Whackers*, fill in the Venn Diagram.

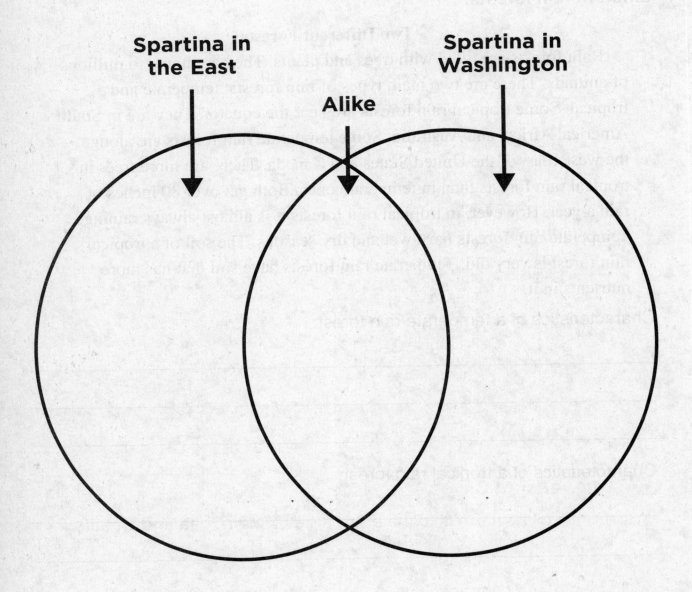

**Spartina in
the East**

Alike

**Spartina in
Washington**

How does the information you wrote in this Venn Diagram help you
monitor comprehension in *Washington Weed Whackers*?

At Home: Have your child use the chart to retell the story.

© Macmillan/McGraw-Hill

Name _____

As I read, I will pay attention to my pronunciation of vocabulary words and other difficult words.

	Oil is found underground. A long drill digs a deep hole
11	to find the oil. The drill must pass through layers of sand
23	and rock.
25	The energy and products we get from oil make our
35	lives easier. But drilling, transporting, and using oil can
44	hurt the environment.
47	At times forests are cut down to run oil pipes under the
59	ground. Huge tankers transport oil. If the oil spills, it can
70	harm **native** fish and sea birds.
76	When oil is burned as fuel in cars or to heat our homes,
89	it gives off gases that pollute the air. **Research** on cars
100	that run on other types of fuel may change that.
110	Another source of energy, natural gas, is used to
119	cook food and to heat homes and water. Pockets of this gas
131	are trapped in the rock and soil under great pressure. By
142	getting at this trapped gas and bringing it to the surface,
153	we can use it for energy. 159

Comprehension Check

1. How can oil be harmful to the environment? **Main Idea and Details**

2. Compare and contrast oil and natural gas. **Compare and Contrast**

	Words Read	−	Number of Errors	=	Words Correct Score
First Read		−		=	
Second Read		−		=	

At Home: Help your child read the passage, paying attention to the goal at the top of the page.

Washington Weed Whackers
Book 3.2/Unit 4   129

Name _____

**How would you research the following topics? On the lines
after each topic, write the various steps you would use to
do research on the computer in your school's media center.
Remember to include key words you would put into the
search engine.**

1. Protecting the beaches of California:

_____

_____

2. Pollution in the Gulf of Mexico:

_____

_____

3. Rain forest preservation in South America:

_____

_____

4. Endangered desert plants in New Mexico:

_____

_____

5. Saving wildlife in the Chesapeake Bay:

_____

_____

6. What is your favorite way to do research on a topic?

_____

At Home: Discuss with your child the different ways of
searching for information in the computer age.

**Make as many contractions as you can, using each word
below as the first part of a contraction. After you write each
contraction, write the two words from which it is formed.
Use the example for help.**

they	should	do	I	we

Example: <u>they'll</u>　　<u>they will</u>

_____　_____　　_____　_____

_____　_____　　_____　_____

_____　_____　　_____　_____

**Write a short conversation between two people about helping the
environment. Have one speaker use several of the contractions
you made. Have the other person speak without using any
contractions.**

_____

_____

_____

_____

_____

_____

_____

At Home: Ask your child to write a definition of
contractions in his or her own words.

Read the words in the box below. Use at least four of the words
with the soft *c* or *g* sound in a paragraph.

danger	custom	general	century	gypsy
gym	genius	twice	place	coal
gentle	celebrate	giant	message	

_____

_____

_____

_____

_____

_____

_____

_____

_____

_____

_____

_____

_____

_____

At Home: Have your child say or write sentences that
contain either a soft *c* or *g* sound (circle, gemstone, circus,
giraffe, icicle) word.

© Macmillan/McGraw-Hill

Name _____

Use the words in the box to complete the puzzle.

| community | deserve | grownups | interviewed |
| slogan | thrilled | tour | volunteers |

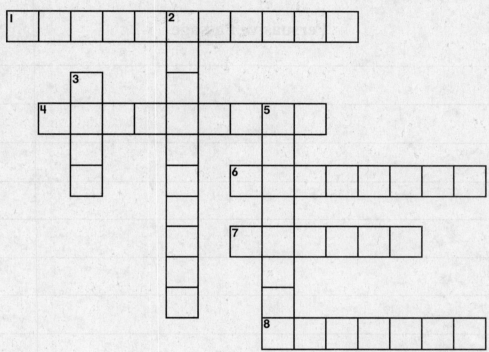

Across

1. asked questions of someone to get information

4. a group of people or animals that live in the same place

6. adults

7. a phrase or motto

8. to have a right to

Down

2. offers to do something, usually without expecting payment

3. a trip or journey to a place

5. gave a feeling of pleasure or excitement

**Read the informative passage below. Then change it to
make it a passage that is persuasive.**

Volunteers will meet after school in the cafeteria. We will discuss ways
to raise money for the library. After our discussion, we will vote on the
suggestions. We will agree to do the project that gets the most votes. Then
everyone will decide what he or she can do to make the project a success.

Persuasive Passage

_____

_____

_____

_____

_____

_____

_____

_____

_____

_____

_____

_____

_____

© Macmillan/McGraw-Hill

At Home: Help your child find an entertaining article in a
newspaper. Discuss the author's purpose. Then challenge
your child to change the article to make it an informative one.

Name _____

As you read *Here's My Dollar*, fill in the Author's Purpose Chart.

Clues

↓

Author's Purpose

How does the information you wrote in this Author's Purpose Chart help you monitor comprehension in *Here's My Dollar*?

 At Home: Have your child use the chart to retell the story.

Here's My Dollar **135**
Book 3.2/Unit 4

© Macmillan/McGraw-Hill

As I read, I will pay attention to tempo.

	The history of service dogs began near the end of
10	World War I. Dogs were trained to guide soldiers who had
20	lost their eyesight. These animals were called guide dogs.
29	During World War II many Americans gave up their
37	dogs so the dogs could defend their country. These former
47	pet dogs kept watch around the beaches and airfields
56	looking for spies. Some went with the troops overseas.
65	They carried notes and guarded army camps at night.
74	Trainers were surprised by the many things dogs could
83	learn to do. Guide dogs can guide their owners away
93	from construction sites or other dangers. The dogs know
102	when it is safe to cross the street.
110	Soon, people learned that dogs could help people in
119	many ways. Today, service dogs are being trained by
128	**volunteers** to do even more to help people. 136

Comprehension Check

1. How did dogs help during World War II? **Summarize**

2. How do guide dogs help blind people? **Main Idea and Details**

	Words Read	–	Number of Errors	=	Words Correct Score
First Read		–		=	
Second Read		–		=	

© Macmillan/McGraw-Hill

At Home: Help your child read the passage, paying attention to the goal at the top of the page.

A. Underline the rhyming words in this poem. Draw a circle around each refrain.

I saw you toss the kites on high
And blow the birds about the sky;
And all around I heard you pass,
Like ladies' skirts across the grass—
  O wind, a-blowing all day long,
  O wind, that sings so loud a song!
O you that are so strong and cold,
O blower, are you young or old?
Are you a beast of field and tree,
Or just a stronger child than me?
  O wind, a-blowing all day long,
  O wind, that sings so loud a song!
        —Robert Louis Stevenson

B. Write a short poem about helping others. Rhyme every other line. Use a refrain.

_____

_____

_____

_____

_____

_____

_____

_____

At Home: Ask your child to write a poem about
something in nature, maybe a poem about snow or rain,
or a particular plant or animal.

Here's My Dollar 137
Book 3.2/Unit 4

Write a sentence for each word below. Include example clues. Use a dictionary if you need help.

1. contemplate: _____

_____

_____

2. senior: _____

_____

_____

3. organization: _____

_____

_____

4. participate: _____

_____

_____

5. improved: _____

_____

_____

At Home: Have your child look up the words *deciduous* and *coniferous* in the dictionary. Then ask them to give examples of each.

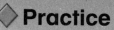

Name _____

Read each pair of homophone. Write a sentence using both.

weight wait	groan grown	tale tail
it's its	pear pair	red read

1. _____

   _____

2. _____

   _____

3. _____

   _____

4. _____

   _____

5. _____

   _____

6. _____

   _____

© Macmillan/McGraw-Hill

At Home: Tell your child a riddle in which the answer is a
homophone for a clue word. For example, "You may see me
when you are on a boat. What am I?" (the sea)

A. An author is writing a story, but she cannot think of the right words. Help the author tell the story by writing the word from the box that makes sense on each line. Use each word only once.

> ruined   storage   crate   determination   exact   separate   luckiest

Shana has decided that she really wants a place of her own. She needs

a _____ space inside the house or in the garage to practice

her music. And Shana is acting with great _____ to get it!

Shana loves to play the drums. She thinks she's the _____

person in the world to be a drummer. Her drums were packed in a

wooden box or _____ when Shana's family moved to

their new house. The drums have stayed in a _____ room

until the family settles into the house. Shana can't wait for the

_____ moment when she can unpack the drums. She is

relieved when she finally does unpack them. The drums are fine. They

have not been _____ during the move. Best of all, Shana

gets her own space in the garage to practice her music!

B. Use two of the vocabulary words in a sentence.

_____

_____

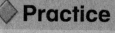
Write your prediction of what will happen next in the story below.

Maya just found out she is going to have a room of her own. Her mom told Maya that she can have some old furniture for her room if she cleans it up and paints it. One Saturday, Maya changes into old clothes and gathers some rags. What will she probably do next?

Prediction: _____

_____

_____

After the furniture is painted, Maya decides to start cleaning the room. She scrubbed the walls and got rid of all the spider webs in the corners. She swept the floor and threw out all the garbage she collected. She then mops the floor with soap and water until it is clean and shines.

Prediction: _____

_____

_____

© Macmillan/McGraw-Hill

At Home: With your child, recite the rhyme, "Jack and Jill." Ask what Jack and Jill will probably do next time they go up the hill—and why.

My Very Own Room • **Book 3.2/Unit 4** ◆ **141**

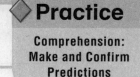

Name _____

As you read *My Very Own Room*, fill in the Predictions Chart.

What I Predict	What Happens

How does the information you wrote in this Predictions Chart help you monitor comprehension in *My Very Own Room*?

At Home: Have your child use the chart to retell the story.

Name _____

As I read, I will pay attention to dialogue.

	"It's time to get ready for the science fair," Ms. Thomas, the
12	science teacher, announced to the science club. "But this year, we'll
23	work in teams, rather than each on your own."
32	"How many teams?" Erin asked.
37	"Let's see," Ms. Thomas said. "There will be five teams, each with
49	three members."
51	"That's only five exhibits," said Ari.
57	"How are we going to pick the teams?" Tanya asked.
67	"We'll pick names out of a hat," Ms. Thomas said.
77	Soon everyone was part of a team.
84	"The fair is in two weeks," Ms. Thomas said. "With hard work and
97	determination, you'll all be done in time. There will be a prize for the
111	best exhibit."
113	"What's the prize?" Ari asked.
118	"I'll keep that as a surprise," Ms. Thomas said. "I predict that this
131	year's fair will be our best yet."
138	Tanya, Erin, and Ari, who were on the same team, met in
150	the school cafeteria.
153	"Who has an idea for the exhibit?" Tanya asked. 162

Comprehension Check

1. What is the science club preparing for? **Main Idea and Details**

2. How many students will participate in the science fair? **Make Inferences**

	Words Read	−	Number of Errors	=	Words Correct Score
First Read		−		=	
Second Read		−		=	

At Home: Help your child read the passage, paying attention to the goal at the top of the page.

Name _____

**Create the first page of an encyclopedia article about castles.
Fill in the missing features below. Use the box to illustrate your
encyclopedia article about castles.**

Page number: _____

Guide word: _____

Heading: _____

Subheading: _____

Castles were built in the Middle Ages
to protect kings and lords from their
enemies. Lords and kings also used
castles to attack and take over land
they wanted. They used castles to
control the new areas they conquered.

Subheading:

_____

_____

Castles were built in stages. First, the   Caption: _____
outer walls went up, then the castle
so the king could rule. After that, the   _____
cathedral was built. This took a long
time because the church was very important to people and the king
wanted it to look beautiful. After the cathedral was finished, the common
people could build their homes. An entire castle could take many, many
years to finish.

Subheading: _____

_____

At Home: Ask your child to explain the difference
between locating information in a set of encyclopedias
and in an online encyclopedia.

Use the picture as a guide as you write a fantasy short story about a bear cub who wanted a room of his own in the family den. Use as many words in the box as you can.

big	young	loud	happy	nice
bigger	younger	louder	happier	nicer
biggest	youngest	loudest	happiest	nicest

_____

_____

_____

_____

_____

_____

_____

At Home: Ask your child to tell you a short story that includes the words *small, smaller, smallest, long, longer,* and *longest.*

Use the plural form of each word to complete the puzzle.

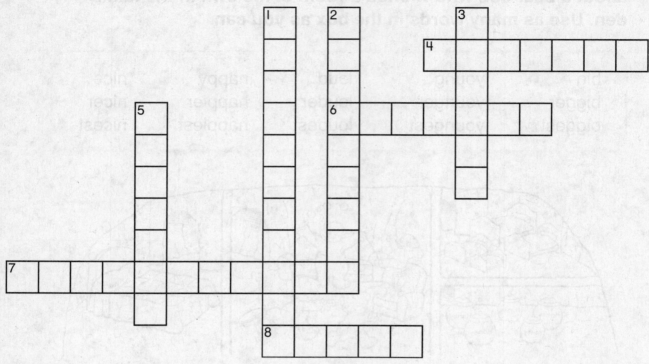

Across

4. daisy

6. penny

7. butterfly

8. sky

Down

1. dragonfly

2. company

3. baby

5. bunny

Use one of the plural words in a sentence that tells why someone might want to have a place of his or her own.

_____

_____

_____

At Home: Ask your child to write the plural form of the words *pony, party,* and *country*. Invite your child to use the words to tell you a short story.

Name _____

You are writing a glossary. Add the missing words or definitions to the entries started below.

recipes	tasty	masterpiece	ingredient	purchased
beamed	research	sprout	native	crate

beamed: _____

_____

_____ : a box for shipping or storing things

_____ : one of the parts in a mixture

masterpiece: _____

_____

native: _____

_____

_____ :bought

_____ :lists of ingredients and instructions for making
something to eat or drink

research: _____

sprout: _____

tasty: _____

Fill in the blanks with the vocabulary words that match the underlined synonyms.

argued	exact	grownups	determination	possessions
storage	clumps	slogan	community	volunteers

1. All the children were outside playing in the yard while the <u>adults</u> or

   _____ were talking inside the house.

2. I packed all my <u>belongings</u> or _____ in boxes before we
   moved to the new house.

3. The coach and the referee <u>quarreled</u> or _____ about
   the goal.

4. The <u>precise</u> or _____ number of people at the game
   was 2,453.

5. All the swimming pool supplies were in the <u>store room</u> or

   _____.

6. While walking towards the beach, we saw <u>bunches</u> or

   _____ of grass.

7. The unpaid <u>workers</u> or _____ did a great job of cleaning
   up the park.

8. Everyone agreed that we needed to do more to clean up our <u>society</u> or

   _____.

9. The new restaurant needed a clever <u>saying</u> or _____ to
   help attract customers.

10. We could see the soccer player's sense of <u>purpose</u> or

    _____ when he went out onto the field.

© Macmillan/McGraw-Hill

Name ____

Write the correct definition as a clue for each vocabulary word in the puzzle.

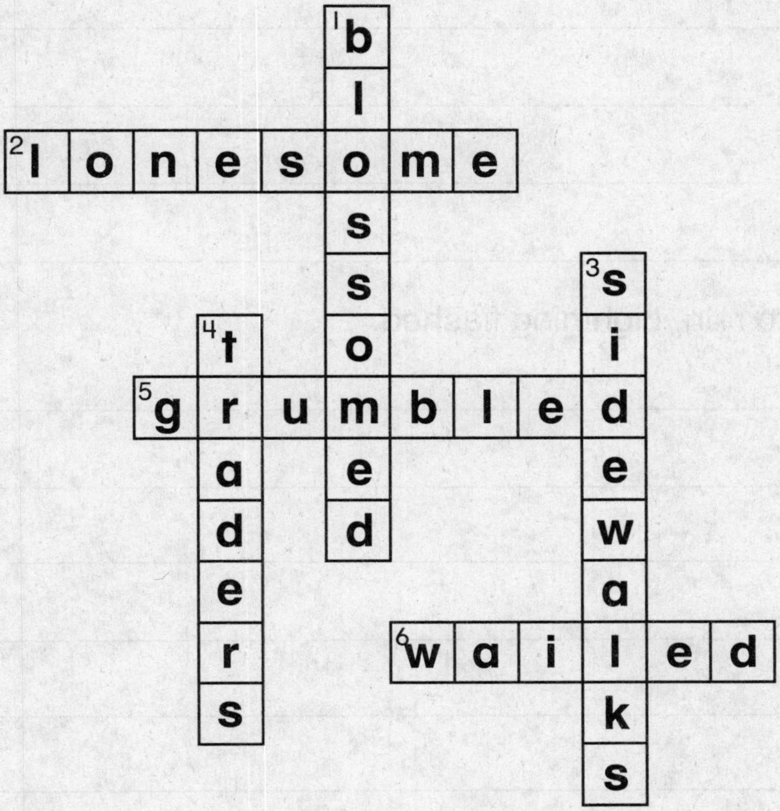
1 blossomed
2 lonesome
3 sidewalks
4 traders
5 grumbled
6 wailed

Across

2. ____

____

5. ____

____

6. ____

____

Down

1. ____

____

3. ____

____

4. ____

____

Read the two events below and think of events before and after them, then write them in the spaces provided. Make the events about working or making money.

1. _____

_____

_____

_____

2. Then it began to rain. Lightning flashed.

3. _____

_____

_____

_____

4. _____

_____

_____

_____

5. Jake woke up and looked out the window.

6. _____

_____

_____

_____

At Home: Ask your child to tell you about his or her day in the sequence that things happened.

As you read *Boom Town*, fill in the Sequence Chart.

Sequence Chart

Event

↓

Event

Sequence Chart

Event

↓

Event

↓

Event

↓

Event

↓

Event

How does the information you wrote in this Sequence Chart help you summarize *Boom Town*?

At Home: Have your child use the chart to retell the story.

Boom Town • **Book 3.2/Unit 5** 151

As I read, I will pay attention to punctuation.

	In the 1890s, cities were booming. Many immigrants lived in
9	tenements. They got jobs in nearby factories and mills where iron
20	and steel was produced or factories that made thread, fabric, clothing,
31	and other goods.
34	The work was long and hard and wages were low. The workrooms
46	were dimly lit and crowded. People grew tired and often grumbled
57	about their jobs. They worked long hours, and there were often
68	accidents and fires.
71	By 1880 there was a great need for steel. Steel is made
82	from iron ore that is found in the earth. Many miners were
94	needed to dig out the iron. That was hard work. Miners
105	worked long hours for little pay. Young boys were paid
115	even less.
117	Coal was also important in the early 1900s. It provided
126	most of the country's energy. Miners worked hundreds of
135	feet below the surface of the earth to dig it out.
146	Both iron and coal miners helped our country to grow. Iron
157	was used for buildings, railroads, and other goods. Coal kept
167	people warm and fueled steam engines. 173

Comprehension Check

1. What does the word wages mean? **Context Clues**

2. Why were young boys paid less? **Make Inferences**

	Words Read	−	Number of Errors	=	Words Correct Score
First Read		–		=	
Second Read		–		=	

© Macmillan/McGraw-Hill

At Home: Help your child read the passage, paying attention to the goal at the top of the page.

Create a calendar for your business. Enter the month and the dates. Decide what business you are interested in starting. Then fill in the calendar boxes with the steps you need to take to start up the business. What research will you do? When? How many days will you advertise? What meetings will you need to set up? What date will you open for business?

My business will be

_____

_____

At Home: Have your child share with you the calendar he or she created. Ask your child questions about the calendar.

Name _____

Write a dialogue between two people who are in the same
business. Use at least six of the compound words in the box.
Use a dictionary if you need help with word meanings.
Underline the words.

bookcase	briefcase	photocopies	mousepad
desktop	salesperson	outlet	stockroom
paperwork	payroll	payday	screensaver

_____

_____

_____

_____

_____

_____

_____

_____

_____

_____

_____

_____

© Macmillan/McGraw-Hill

At Home: Together, make a list of items in your home that
can be put together to make compound words (cookbook,
bookcase, staircase, stepladder).

Name _____

Use the words in the box to form four compound words.
Then make up four riddles in which the answer is one of the
compound words.

boy	cab	clerk	note
dress	black	cow	driver
maker	sales	smith	book

Compound Words:

1. _____   3. _____

2. _____   4. _____

Riddle 1

_____

_____

_____

_____

Riddle 2

_____

_____

_____

_____

Riddle 3

_____

_____

_____

_____

Riddle 4

_____

_____

_____

_____

At Home: Together with your child, tell some riddles, jokes,
and puns that use compound words.

Name _____

Use vocabulary words to fill in the missing letters in the crossword puzzle below. Then write the correct definition as a clue for each vocabulary word.

Across

5. _____
_____

6. _____
_____

7. _____
_____

Down

1. _____
_____

2. _____
_____

3. _____
_____

4. _____

© Macmillan/McGraw-Hill

Complete each sentence with either a cause or an effect. Then underline the cause and circle the effect.

1. Mr. Gonzales fixed his fence because _____

_____

_____

2. James watched his little brother and sister so _____

_____

_____

3. As a result of the students cleaning the park, _____

_____

_____

4. Since I am the coach, _____

_____

_____

5. Many students began to volunteer at the library because _____

_____

_____

6. The gardener planted trees so _____

_____

_____

At Home: Discuss with your child how after school sports, clubs, or music lessons could affect his or her daily schedule.

Name _____

As you read *Beatrice's Goat,* fill in the Cause and Effect Chart.

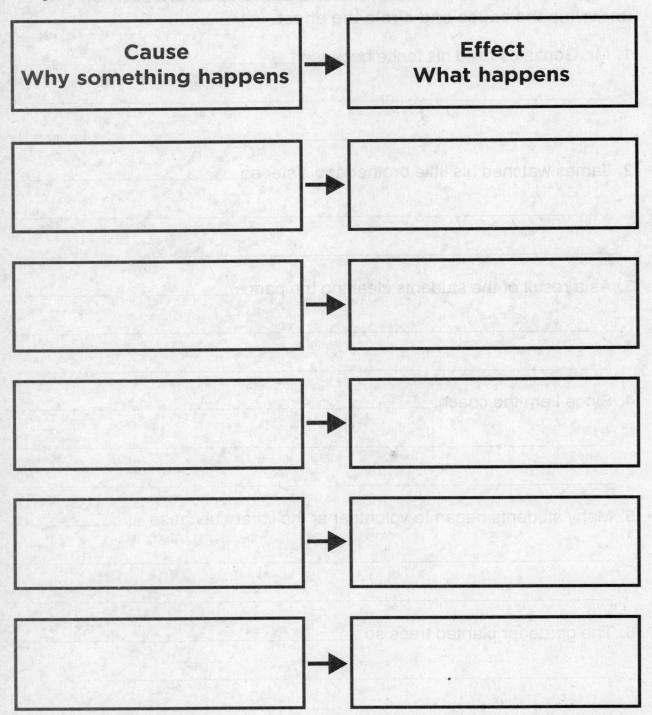

Cause Why something happens	Effect What happens

How does the information you wrote in this Cause and Effect Chart help you make inferences and analyze *Beatrice's Goat*?

© Macmillan/McGraw-Hill

At Home: Have your child use the chart to retell the story.

As I read, I will pay attention to genre of the passage.

9	Alexander Fleming was born in 1881. He grew up on a farm in a remote part of Scotland. As a schoolboy, he
21	walked barefoot to a country schoolhouse miles away.
29	When not in school or tending sheep, he and his three
40	brothers would play outdoors.
44	When Fleming was in his teens, his family moved to
54	London. London was a crowded, noisy place. Fleming's
62	new home was over an underground railway. Every few
71	minutes the sturdy house would shake as a steam train
81	roared below.
83	Think about moving from a quiet, peaceful farm, to a
93	big city. Fleming and his brothers loved it. To them, it
104	probably felt like going from a desert island to the middle
115	of a fun fair.
119	Fleming left school at age 16 and went to work in an
130	office. He had to copy piles of letters and business forms
141	by hand. He did this for long hours, six days a week. He
154	yearned for another type of work. 160

Comprehension Check

1. What was Alexander Fleming's childhood like? **Summarize**

2. How was Fleming's life different in London? **Compare and Contrast**

	Words Read	−	Number of Errors	=	Words Correct Score
First Read		−		=	
Second Read		−		=	

At Home: Help your child read the passage, paying attention to the goal at the top of the page.

Name _____

**Think about a change in your school that could improve
the building or something else about your school. How
could you convince your classmates to help make that
change? Write a persuasive editorial in the space below.
Be sure to include examples or evidence.**

_____

_____

_____

_____

_____

_____

_____

_____

_____

_____

_____

_____

_____

_____

_____

© Macmillan/McGraw-Hill

At Home: Look at the editorial page of the local newspaper
with your child. Discuss the ways that the editorials try to
persuade readers.

A. Use the word parts in the box to make new words from the base words listed below. Then write a sentence using one of the new words in each word family.

re	every	ing	ion	room	mate	ship	some

1. direct _____

_____

2. friend _____

_____

3. class _____

_____

4. help _____

_____

5. one _____

_____

6. try _____

_____

B. Write new words for the base words below.

7. understand _____

8. place _____

At Home: Take turns with your child combining two word parts from the base words *every, some, no, one, body,* and *where* to make as many words as possible.

Beatrice's Goat • **Book 3.2/Unit 5** 161

◆ **Practice**

**Phonics:
Words with Inflected
Endings**

**A. Circle the word with an inflected ending and write whether the
tense is past or present.**

1. Jiwon traded her pen for a pencil. _____

2. Tristan helps his mother with dinner. _____

3. We are voting for class president. _____

4. Stephanie clapped when she heard the good news.

_____

5. Hector is caring for the ducks. _____

6. Kristen mopped the floors yesterday. _____

7. Fluffy marshmallows topped my hot chocolate. _____

8. Evan zips his parka up to go outside. _____

9. Diego is juggling several projects at the same time. _____

10. Mia brushes her hair early in the morning. _____

**B. Have students identify each of the base words from above
and use two of them in a sentence.**

11. Base Words: _____

_____

12. Sentence: _____

_____

At Home: Ask your child to tell you a few sentences
that use different inflected endings with the base words
from the activity.

© Macmillan/McGraw-Hill

Name _____

Do you like to travel by bike, car, train, airplane? Use all of the vocabulary words to write a paragraph describing your favorite way to travel. Include a title for your paragraph.

powered	declared	artist's	existed	pride

_____

_____

_____

_____

_____

_____

_____

_____

_____

_____

Read each sentence about different kinds of transportation.
On the first blank line, write whether the sentence is a fact or an
opinion. If the sentence is a fact, write a new sentence that is an
opinion about the same kind of transportation. If the sentence is
an opinion, write a fact.

1. Trucks haul goods across the country.

_____

_____

_____

2. Airplanes have two wings.

_____

_____

_____

3. The best way to see the country is to travel by bus.

_____

_____

_____

4. I think riding a bicycle along a country road is boring.

_____

_____

_____

© Macmillan/McGraw-Hill

At Home: Ask your child to tell you one fact and one opinion
about a way to travel that was not on this page, such as a
car, boat, or skateboard.

Name _____

As you read *A Carousel of Dreams*, fill in the Fact and Opinion Chart.

Fact	Opinion

How does the information you wrote in this Fact and Opinion Chart help you make inferences and analyze *A Carousel of Dreams*?

At Home: Have your child use the chart to retell the story.

A Carousel of Dreams
Book 3.2/Unit 5

165

Name _____

As I read, I will pay attention to my pronunciation of vocabulary words and other difficult words.

	Drawbridges came into use when castles were first built in England
11	after 1066. This was about thirty years before the time of knights in
23	shining armor. People who lived in these castles owned the land around
35	them for many miles. Castles **existed** as forts to protect this land. From
48	the highest part of the castle, they could see if someone was trying to
62	invade their land.
65	If attacked, those who lived in the castle could defend themselves in
77	several ways. Standing at the top of the castle, they could shoot arrows at
91	their enemies. They could also use a drawbridge. Moats surrounded many
102	castles, and the only way to cross them was to use the drawbridge. When
116	the castle was threatened, someone inside would turn a winch that worked
128	a pulley. This pulley pulled a chain attached to the drawbridge. The
140	drawbridge would turn on a pivot and lift up.
149	In our time, drawbridges let tall ships pass through a waterway. Modern
161	drawbridges use a light sensor to tell when a ship or boat is near. 175

Comprehension Check

1. How did moats and drawbridges protect castles? **Summarize**

2. How are the first drawbridges different from drawbridges today?
Compare and Contrast

	Words Read	−	Number of Errors	=	Words Correct Score
First Read		−		=	
Second Read		−		=	

At Home: Help your child read the passage, paying attention to the goal at the top of the page.

© Macmillan/McGraw-Hill

A. Skim and scan the passage to answer the following questions. Write the answer on the line below each question.

During the 1800s several women were responsible for transportation related inventions. Mary I. Riggin invented the railway crossing gate. Eliza Murfey invented lubricating systems for railroad car axles. Her inventions helped to prevent trains from going off the tracks.

Women's contributions to transportation continued into the 1900s. In 1903 Mary Anderson invented a windshield wiper for early automobiles. In 1911 Harriet Quimby became the first woman pilot. In 1921 Bessie Coleman became the first African American woman pilot. One of the most famous women pilots was Amelia Earhart. In 1932 she became the first woman to fly across the Atlantic Ocean.

1. What is a good title for this passage? _____

_____

2. To answer question 1, should you skim or scan the passage? Explain

your answer. _____

_____

_____

B. Write two questions that can be answered by skimming or scanning the passage.

3. Question: _____

Answer: _____

4. Question: _____

Answer: _____

At Home: Ask your child to scan a newspaper article and then tell you what the article was about. Then ask what key words helped your child form a summary.

Name _____

**Write two different sentences with each word as a possessive.
Use the word as a singular noun in the first sentence and as a
plural noun in the second sentence.**

1. bike _____

_____

_____

2. train _____

_____

_____

3. plane _____

_____

_____

4. ship _____

_____

_____

5. truck _____

_____

_____

© Macmillan/McGraw-Hill

At Home: Ask your child to write a sentence for each
of the following nouns in their possessive forms: *boy,
dogs, car, women.*

**Write a sentence for each word below and add inflected endings
_s, -ed,_ or _-ing_ to the word.**

1. rely _____

_____

2. spy _____

_____

3. apply _____

_____

4. deny _____

_____

5. delay _____

_____

6. fry _____

_____

7. hurry _____

_____

8. satisfy _____

_____

At Home: Give your child a list of words and have him or her
write three sentences, one with the base word, one using the
word with _-s_ or _-ed,_ and the third using the word with _-ing._

**Write a short newspaper article that describes a heroes actions.
Use all the words from the box in your article.**

fled	screamed	numb	escape
shuddered	image	newspaper	

_____

_____

_____

_____

_____

_____

_____

_____

_____

_____

_____

_____

_____

© Macmillan/McGraw-Hill

A. Make a prediction based on information you read in the paragraph below.

Kendra's grandmother was her hero. Gramma was a lawyer. She helped people who didn't have much money to pay for lawyers. Yesterday Jeff called Gramma. He was trying to get permission to clean up a city park and put in playground equipment. Jeff needed a lawyer to fill out complicated forms and file them with the city. Jeff didn't have much money to pay a lawyer. What will probably happen next? Why?

Prediction:_____

_____

_____

B. Write a short paragraph that provides clues that lead to the prediction below.

Passage: _____

_____

_____

_____

_____

_____

_____

Prediction: Aaron helped Mrs. Smith and carried her groceries to her
home for her.

At Home: Ask your child how predicting the weather is like predicting what will happen in a story.

The Printer • **Book 3.2/Unit 5** 171

Name _____

As you read *The Printer*, fill in the Predictions Chart.

Predictions Chart

What I Predict	What Happens

How does the information you wrote in this Predictions Chart help you make inferences and analyze *The Printer*?

 At Home: Have your child use the chart to retell the story.

© Macmillan/McGraw-Hill

Name _____

As I read, I will pay attention to punctuation.

	We know a lot of things about earthquakes. We know
10	what causes them and where they are likely to happen. We
21	know what to do to be prepared.
28	However, we cannot tell when an earthquake will hit or
38	how big it will be. We have to be ready for anything. We
51	must rely on earthquake heroes to help us.
59	Earthquake heroes work before, during, and after
66	an earthquake. They try to make sure that people are safe
77	and property is protected.
81	Some earthquake heroes are on the job even before an
91	earthquake strikes. A scientist who studies earthquakes
98	is called a seismologist. Seismologists are part of a team
108	of earthquake heroes. They work in labs and in the field
119	to learn how energy moves through rock. They watch
128	how Earth's crust moves. They keep track of where
137	and when quakes occur. They measure how strong the
146	quakes are. 148

Comprehension Check

1. What do we know about earthquakes? **Main Idea and Details**

2. What are seismologists and what do they do? **Summarize**

	Words Read	–	Number of Errors	=	Words Correct Score
First Read		–		=	
Second Read		–		=	

At Home: Help your child read the passage, paying attention to the goal at the top of the page.

Name _____

You're a hero to hikers because you're an excellent mapmaker. Follow the instructions in the box to create a map. Be sure to include a compass rose and a map key.

1. Use symbols for lake, forest, hills, town, and campground.

2. Show the lake north of the forest.

3. Show the hills to the east of the lake.

4. Show the town north of the forest and east of the hills.

5. Show the campground west of the town and south of the lake.

MAP KEY

6. Write directions for a hiker to travel from the hills to the campground.

_____

_____

_____

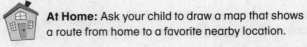

At Home: Ask your child to draw a map that shows a route from home to a favorite nearby location.

© Macmillan/McGraw-Hill

**Use at least four examples of figurative language from
the box to explain why a friend, family member, or teacher
is a hero. Underline each example of figurative language.**

the cool breath of winter	ran like the wind
sea of people	the world is a stage
strong as an ox	as tall as a mountain
brave as a lion	quick as a wink
wise as an owl	like a bowl of cherries
crying a flood of tears	

_____

_____

_____

_____

_____

_____

_____

_____

_____

At Home: Ask your child to use three examples of
figurative language to tell about the characters and plot
of a favorite story.

Name _____

| better | follow | welcome | always |

A. Write each word from the box and divide it into syllables.
Write *VC/CV* to show the pattern of vowel-consonant-consonant-vowel.

_____   _____

_____   _____

B. Write four riddles. The answer to each riddle should be
a word that has the *VC/CV* pattern.

_____   _____

_____   _____

_____   _____

What am I?   What am I?

_____   _____

_____   _____

_____   _____

What am I?   What am I?

_____   _____

© Macmillan/McGraw-Hill

At Home: Ask your child to draw a line to divide the words
cellar and *basket* into syllables, and write the letters VCCV to
show the pattern in each word.

Name _____

Look at the crossword puzzle. Some of the answers have been given. Some clues have been provided. Complete the crossword and fill in the missing clues.

```
¹ |  |²r|  |  |  |  |  |  |³c|  |⁴ |
      |e|                    |o|   |  |
      |t|              ⁵s     |n|   |  |
      |r|               t     |t|   |  |
   ⁶ |  |e|  |  |  |  |  |r|   |a|   |
      |a|               u     |i|   |
      |t|               c     |n|   |  |
      |s|               t
                        u
                        r
                        e
      ⁷ |  |  |  |  |  |s|
```

Across

1. people who plan and design houses and other buildings

6. a structure that protects

7. where bees live

Down

2. _____

3. _____

4. not deep

5. _____

A. Read the passage below. Write five details about a magpie's nest on the lines that follow the passage.

The Magpie

The magpie is a type of bird. It uses twigs and mud to make its nest. The magpie finds shiny objects to keep in its nest. Its nest may have bits of wire, tiny metal ties, and even coat hangers. If you lose a shiny ring, the magpie may grab it with its beak. Watch out for your coins, too!

Details: _____

_____

B. Write a paragraph describing an animal's home that you've seen in a zoo or in your community.

_____

_____

_____

_____

_____

_____

_____

_____

_____

_____

© Macmillan/McGraw-Hill

At Home: Have your child research an animal habitat.

Name _____

As you read *Animal Homes*, fill in the Description Web.

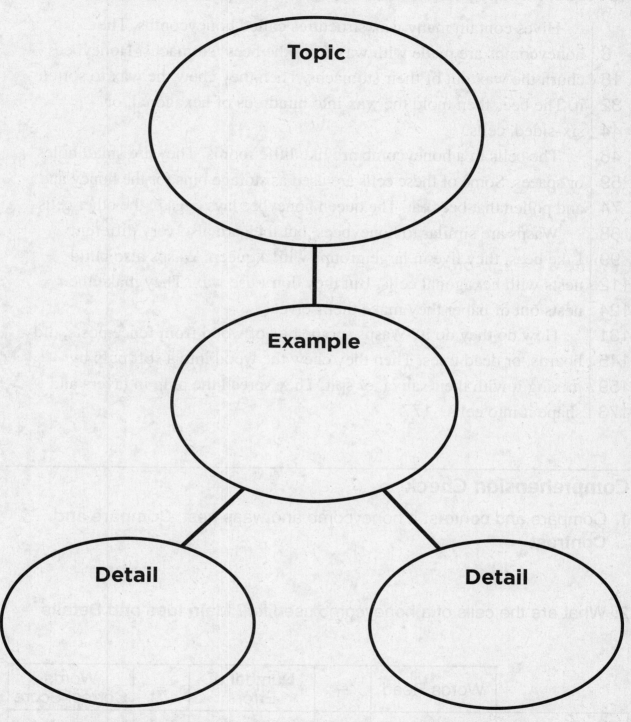

How does the information you wrote in this Description Web help you
summarize *Animal Homes*?

At Home: Have your child use the chart to retell the story.

Animal Homes • **Book 3.2/Unit 5** ◆ 179

As I read, I will pay attention to the genre of the passage.

	Hives contain many wax structures called honeycombs. The
8	honeycombs are made with wax from the bees' stomachs. Honeybees
18	churn the wax out of their stomachs. Then they chew the wax to soften
32	it. The bees then mold the wax into hundreds of hexagonal, or
44	six-sided, cells.
46	The cells in a honeycomb are like little rooms. They are small holes
59	or spaces. Some of these cells are used as storage bins for the honey and
74	and pollen that bees eat. The queen honeybee lays eggs in the other cells.
88	Wasps are similar to honeybees, but they are also very different.
99	Like bees, they live in large groups with a queen. Wasps also build
112	nests with hexagonal cells. But they don't use wax. They make their
124	nests out of paper they make themselves!
131	How do they do it? Wasps scrape bits of wood from fence posts, old
145	boards, or dead trees. Then they chew the wood into a soft pulp by
159	mixing it with their saliva, or spit. They spread the pulp in layers and
173	shape it into cells. 177

Comprehension Check

1. Compare and contrast a honeycomb and wasp nest. **Compare and Contrast**

2. What are the cells of a honeycomb used for? **Main Idea and Details**

	Words Read	–	Number of Errors	=	Words Correct Score
First Read		–		=	
Second Read		–		=	

© Macmillan/McGraw-Hill

At Home: Help your child read the passage, paying attention to the goal at the top of the page.

Name _____

A limerick is a funny poem that is five lines long with a specific rhyme and **rhythmic pattern**. Usually the last words in the first, second, and fifth lines rhyme. The third and fourth lines usually rhyme with each other. Some limericks include one or more **similes**.

Write two limericks with an animal theme. Be sure to include a simile and a rhyming pattern in each.

A. _____

_____

_____

_____

_____

B. _____

_____

_____

_____

_____

_____

_____

_____

_____

_____

At Home: Share a few of your child's favorite poems.
Together, look for rhythmic patterns and similes.

Animal Homes • Book 3.2/Unit 5 ◇ 181

A. Fill in the blanks to complete the analogies

1. insect is to spider as bone is to _____

2. bird is to fly as _____ is to _____

3. lodge is to beaver as _____ is to bee

B. Create three analogies about animals. Think of where animals live, what they eat, how they look, and how they behave. Use the words in the box for ideas to get started.

| bird | beaver | lion | kangaroo | den | pocket | nest | cave |

Example:
feather is to **bird** as **fur** is to **lion**

4. _____

_____

5. _____

_____

6. _____

_____

At Home: Have your child decide on a topic, such as animals, and a word relationship, such as antonyms and create an analogy.

A. Sort the two-syllable words in the box below by V/CV or VC/V patterns.

cavern	frozen	robot	camel	level	spider
tiny	shiver	floral	icing	forest	weasel

Long Vowels V/CV

_____

_____

_____

_____

_____

Short Vowels VC/V

_____

_____

_____

_____

_____

B. Rearrange the letters to form a word with the VC/V or V/CV pattern. Show where the word is broken into two syllables.

Example: I T S N A _____

1. I I T S V _____

2. O T O H P _____

3. N N A I O T _____

© Macmillan/McGraw-Hill

At Home: Have your child list words from the kitchen that
have the V/CV and VC/V pattern.

Animal Homes • Book 3.2/Unit 5 **183**

Name _____

A. Draw a line from a word in the first column to a word in the second column to form a compound word. Then write the correct compound word to complete each sentence.

lone	hearted
school	paper
news	house
kind	some

1. My dad reads the _____ every morning.

2. _____ people are usually happy to help others.

3. I was very _____ when we first moved to this town.

4. My mom's first school was a one-room _____ near her farm.

B. Write *true* if the statement below is true. If it is *false*, rewrite the sentence to make it true.

5. If your desk is sturdy, it will wobble. _____

_____

6. If you escape, you become free. _____

7. Architects plan and design buildings. _____

8. A person who retreats moves straight ahead. _____

_____

© Macmillan/McGraw-Hill

A. Write a synonym and an antonym or antonym phrase for each of the words.

1. contain: _____

2. declared: _____

3. existed: _____

4. fled: _____

5. pride: _____

6. retreats: _____

7. sturdy: _____

8. yearned: _____

B. Write a sentence using each of the vocabulary words. Remember to include context clues.

9. numb _____

_____

10. tend _____

_____

11. grumbled _____

_____

14. schoolhouse _____

_____

Name _____

As you read each question below, look at the underlined word, and write your answer. Then write a short definition of the underlined word.

1. What are two <u>appliances</u> that are found in many homes?

   _____

   Definition: _____

2. Where in your home might you find something that is <u>leaky</u>?

   _____

   Definition: _____

3. What kinds of workers might find jobs where <u>construction</u> is taking place?

   _____

   Definition: _____

4. What type of <u>equipment</u> do people who work on a construction site need?

   _____

   Definition: _____

5. What kinds of buildings are in the <u>downtown</u> areas of most cities?

   _____

   Definition: _____

6. What kinds of things might new <u>owners</u> of houses need?

   _____

   Definition: _____

A **theme** is the message the author wants the reader to understand. For example the theme of the fable, "The Tortoise and the Hare," is "Slow and steady wins the race."

Read the passage below and answer the questions that follow.

One weekend I went to visit my aunt and uncle who lived in another town. My uncle was a rock climbing coach for an afterschool program in that town. He offered to take me rock climbing with the other kids in his group. I had never been rock climbing before. I was a little afraid of heights and I was really afraid of looking foolish in front of other kids. I told my fears to my uncle. He told me that he understood my fears, but that I would be safe at all times. I would be connected to a safety harness if I fell. My uncle also pointed out that I shouldn't be worried about looking foolish. The other kids in this group had never rock climbed either. I felt a lot better after I heard this and I looked forward to learning how to rock climb.

1. What do you think is the most important theme of this passage?

_____

_____

2. What theme or message about communication does the passage want the

reader to understand? _____

_____

_____

At Home: Together, think of and discuss the themes of familiar fables.

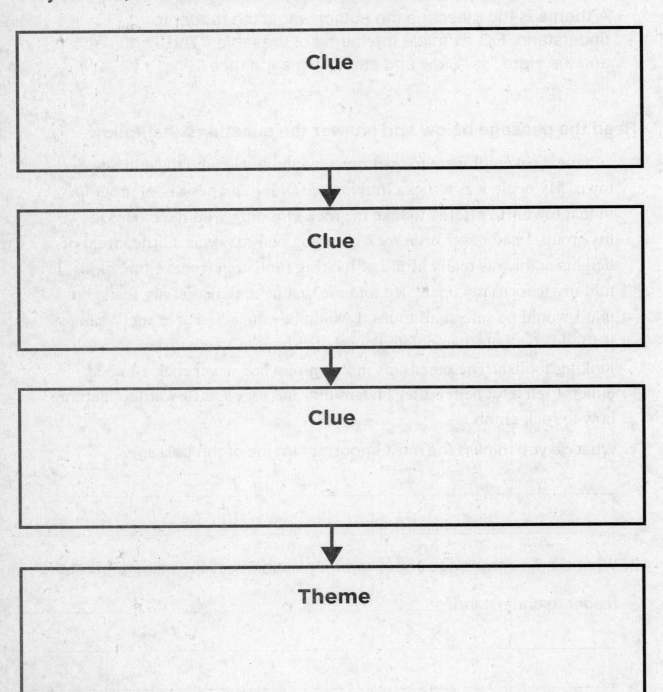

Name _____

As you read, *A Castle on Viola Street,* **fill in the Theme Map.**

Clue

↓

Clue

↓

Clue

↓

Theme

How does the information you wrote in this Theme Map help you
analyze story structure in *A Castle on Viola Street*?

At Home: Have your child use the chart to retell the story.

As I read, I will pay attention to inflection and punctuation.

14	It had been two weeks since his family had moved to Gatesburg. In all that time, Jeremy hadn't met a single kid his own age. In fact, he hadn't
29	met any kids at all.
34	In his old neighborhood, there was always something going on. After
45	school, children brought out their roller skates and bicycles. They played
56	one-on-one at the O'Neills' house. They skateboarded in the school
66	playground.
67	Jeremy hadn't realized that Gatesburg would be so different. It was a
79	brand new suburb and the houses were bigger and farther apart. Some were
92	still under construction. Even the finished homes appeared empty because
102	trees, grass, and flowers hadn't been planted yet. He rarely saw the owners
115	outside. There was hardly any traffic on the streets. And there were no
128	sidewalks either.
130	Jeremy could usually talk to his parents about things that worried him,
142	but lately they hadn't had time to listen. They were preoccupied with
154	getting the house in order. They were busy with chores or dashing out
167	on various errands. 170

Comprehension Check

1. Compare and contrast Jeremy's new neighborhood and old neighborhood. **Compare and Contrast**

2. Why is Jeremy worried? **Draw Conclusions**

	Words Read	–	Number of Errors	=	Words Correct Score
First Read		–		=	
Second Read		–		=	

At Home: Help your child read the passage, paying attention to the goal at the top of the page.

Name _____

Suppose you are writing an article about building an ideal house for a family of six people. The family includes parents, children, and grandparents. Write a short article about your ideas for the house and your plans for getting it built. Include the following features in your article:

- a short introduction that tells what will be discussed in the article

- boldface type to emphasize one or more special words in your introduction

- a heading for the next section of your text

- a small picture with a caption that gives information about the house

_____

_____

_____

_____

_____

_____

_____

_____

_____

At Home: Have your child locate and show you newspaper articles with examples of headings, boldface type, different type sizes, and photographs with captions.

Write sentences about a new home using the words below. Be sure to include clues for the words. Then write the definition of the word.

1. electric _____

_____

Definition: _____

2. bulldozer _____

_____

Definition: _____

3. budget _____

_____

Definition: _____

4. flooring _____

_____

Definition: _____

5. permits _____

_____

Definition: _____

6. model _____

_____

Definition: _____

At Home: With your child, identify the context clues
used in the story.

A Castle on Viola Street
Book 3.2/Unit 6
191

A. Answer each of the questions below with a word from the box that ends with el or le.

nickel	raccoon	squirrel	handle	couple	gavel
jungle	edge	bangle	paler	channel	fringe

1. What is worth five cents? _____

2. What is a small animal with a bushy tail? _____

3. What is the part of a tool that you hold? _____

B. Write similar questions for three other words in the box that end with el or le.

_____

_____

_____

_____

_____

_____

_____

At Home: As you and your child read, have your child point out words that have the final /əl/ sound.

Look at the crossword puzzle. Use the vocabulary words from the box to answer the Across clues. The answers for the Down clues are given, use them to write the clues.

boasting	conversation	interrupted	seized
rebuild	scrambled	sway	

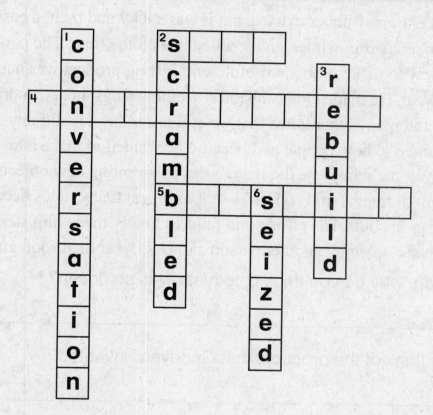

Across

2. to move from side to side

4. stopped from speaking

5. speaking with too much pride

Down

1. _____

2. _____

3. _____

6. _____

When you **make judgments**, it means you form an opinion of a character's actions. Readers should use details from the story and their own experience to support their judgment.

Read the passage and then answer the questions below.

Before 1839, people didn't have good waterproof raincoats, rubber tires, or pencil erasers. Rubber existed, but it was sticky and melted easily in summer, broke apart in winter, and smelled bad all the time. The person who found a way to make rubber a useful, long-lasting product was named Charles Goodyear. He made clothes, babies' teething rings, boats, doormats, electric cords and many other items that we still use today. He did this because he wanted to help people and because he wanted to make a lot of money. However, the money he did make went to inventing new objects instead of supporting his family. He was sent to prison many times because he could not pay his bills. His efforts and failures finally made him sick. Then his idea was stolen by another person and Goodyear died soon after.

1. In your opinion, why do you think Goodyear was so driven?

_____

2. What do you think of the products that Goodyear invented?

_____

3. Do you think Goodyear's efforts were worth the price he paid? Why or

why not? _____

4. How did you reach your judgment? _____

_____

At Home: Have your child think about a time when he or she had to make a judgment about something.

Name _____

As you read *Wilbur's Boast*, fill in the Judgment Chart.

Action	→	Judgment
	→	
	→	

How does the information you wrote in this Judgment Chart help you monitor comprehension in *Wilbur's Boast*?

© Macmillan/McGraw-Hill

At Home: Have your child use the chart to retell the story.

As I read, I will pay attention to punctuation.

	The grizzly bear sat quietly a moment, tapping her chin
10	thoughtfully. "You know," she said at last, "I think it would be a
23	wonderful experience if you were to come fishing with me tomorrow.
34	We can fish together, and you will see for yourself what an expert I am.
49	I do not need any help from a pelican. What do you say?"
62	The frigate bird nodded in agreement. "I would be delighted to go
74	fishing with you," he said. He was sure that the grizzly bear couldn't
87	be as good at fishing as she said she was. He wanted to see her in
103	action. "I will meet you here by the river for breakfast."
114	Early the next morning, the grizzly bear and the frigate bird met up
127	on the rocky land at the mouth of the river that ran into the sea. The
143	grizzly bear stood perched on a big rock overlooking the swirling
154	waters. She looked as graceful as a ballerina standing on tiptoe.
165	The frigate bird always moved awkwardly on land. 173

Comprehension Check

1. Why does the grizzly bear invite the frigate bird to go fishing? **Main Idea and Details**

2. Why does the frigate bird agree to go fishing with the grizzly bear? **Main Idea and Details**

	Words Read	–	Number of Errors	=	Words Correct Score
First Read		–		=	
Second Read		–		=	

© Macmillan/McGraw-Hill

At Home: Help your child read the passage, paying attention to the goal at the top of the page.

Name _____

Directions help you follow steps to do or make something. Directions usually include a list of materials needed for the project and are often numbered or follow bullets.

Below are directions for making an origami butterfly. Answer the questions that follow.

Materials

construction paper, scissors, markers or crayons,
a pipe cleaner or curling ribbon for antennae

1. Start with a square piece of paper.
2. Fold the square in half to make a triangle.
3. Open up the fold you just made. Put the triangle on the table with the central fold pointing up (like a tent). Fold one corner over.
4. Open it up again. Fold the other corner over.
5. Open it up. You now have a butterfly shape.
6. Decorate the butterfly.
7. Attach two antennae made of pipe cleaners or curling ribbon (curled by pulling along a scissors).

1. What do the directions describe?

_____

2. What information tells you what you will need to make the butterfly?

_____

3. How many steps do you have to follow to make the butterfly? _____

4. What other kind of information would be helpful to include with these

directions? _____

At Home: Discuss with your child situations in which giving
or receiving exact directions is necessary.

Wilbur's Boast • Book 3.2/Unit 6 ◇197◇

© Macmillan/McGraw-Hill

Read each sentence. Add the prefix *re-*, *pre-*, *dis-*, or *un-* to a word in the box and then complete each sentence.

covered	design	certain	test
continued	historic	able	appeared

1. I was _____ to check out the book on animals without my library card.

2. We lost the dog's collar and finally _____ it behind his food.

3. My sister is _____ which book she needs from the library.

4. Our dog dug up some bones from the backyard that looked

   _____.

5. The bird that hid behind the branch finally _____ and flew away.

6. The dog got too big for his house so we had to _____ a new one.

7. We were unhappy to learn that the paint we would use for the doghouse

   had been _____.

8. I cannot walk my dog because I am taking a _____ to get ready for tomorrow's test.

© Macmillan/McGraw-Hill

At Home: Together, invent new words by adding prefixes to everyday words. Discuss which of your words make sense and which do not.

Name _____

Prefixes are word parts that are added to the beginning of base words. Prefixes change the meanings of base words.

The sentences below have words with prefixes, but the prefixes are incorrect. Circle the incorrect prefix and then write the word with the correct prefix on the blank line.

1. Some of the fruit is reripe so we should wait for a few days before we eat it. _____

2. Devon was filled with untrust when Kim made a promise she couldn't keep. _____

3. Cara said that it is disusual for her cat to bite anyone. _____

4. Learning to ride a bicycle means that sometimes you will be wobbly and prebalanced. _____

5. Could you prefill that glass so I can have another sip? _____

6. The doctor disscribed a vaccination to keep me from getting sick this winter. _____

7. The rules of our classroom state that we are not allowed to rerespect others. _____

8. My library card is prenewable every year which means I can get a new one on January 1. _____

At Home: Try to have a conversation with your child without using any words that have prefixes. Discuss how much we use prefixes to make ourselves clear.

Wilbur's Boast • **Book 3.2/Unit 6** 199

Name _____

A. Answer each question with a complete sentence that includes the underlined vocabulary word.

1. Where might a <u>dispute</u> be settled legally?

_____

_____

2. What are some <u>requirements</u> for being President of the United States?

_____

_____

3. What is one date that has <u>historical</u> importance? Why?

_____

_____

4. What is one number or group of numbers that most people know <u>automatically</u>?

_____

_____

B. Write a similar question using one of the underlined vocabulary words. Write a possible answer to your question.

5. Question: _____

   Answer: _____

   _____

© Macmillan/McGraw-Hill

Name _____

Good citizens work together to solve problems. Every neighborhood has problems that kids can help solve. Choose one of the ideas below, or come up with one of your own. Write a paragraph explaining how you would solve the problem that you chose.

Possible problems:

- litter on the sidewalks

- kids who are bored after school is over for the day

- older people in the neighborhood who can't get out in stormy weather to shop for food or do errands

_____

_____

_____

_____

_____

_____

_____

_____

_____

At Home: State a solution and ask your child what problem it might solve.

An American Hero Flies Again
Book 3.2/Unit 6 ◇201◇

As you read *An American Hero Flies Again*, fill in the Problem and Solution Chart.

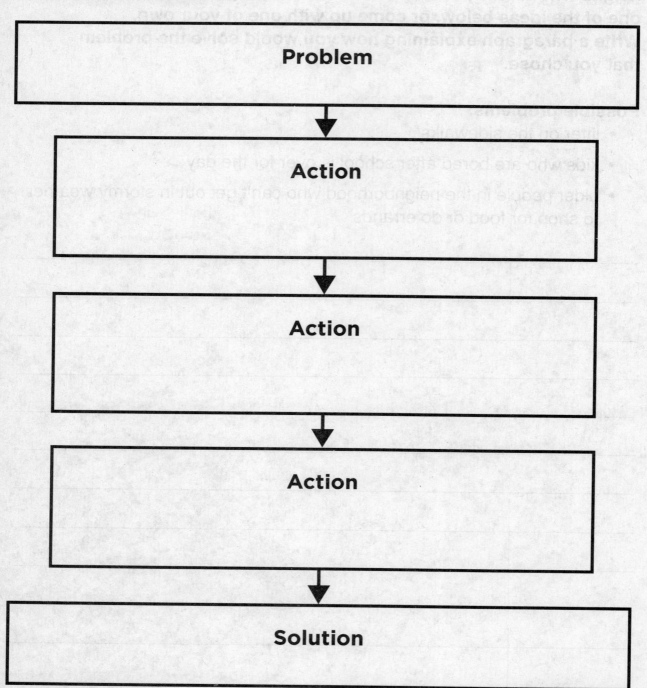

Problem

↓

Action

↓

Action

↓

Action

↓

Solution

How does the information you wrote in the Problem and Solution Chart help you analyze text structure in *An American Hero Flies Again*?

 At Home: Have your child use the chart to retell the story.

As I read, I will pay attention to my pronunciation of vocabulary words and other difficult words.

	Colonial America won its freedom from England in 1783. But there
10	were new problems. The 13 colonies were now 13 united states, and they
21	had to work together. They had **disputes** on many issues. They needed a
34	strong government to bring them together.
40	In May, 1787, a **historical** meeting took place. Men from the newly
51	formed states attended the Constitutional Convention in the city of
61	Philadelphia. They came to work out a new plan of government. George
73	Washington led the meeting. Benjamin Franklin attended and was looked
83	on with great respect. He had worked as a leader for many years.
96	Franklin was one of the founding fathers of the United States. He
108	was also a writer, inventor, diplomat, and statesman. He helped write the
120	Declaration of Independence. He spoke for the United States in France
131	during the war against England.
136	Now, at age 81, Franklin was in poor health. He could not lead the
149	convention. However, he was its voice of wisdom and experience. 159

Comprehension Check

1. Who was Benjamin Franklin? **Main Idea and Details**

2. Why couldn't Benjamin Franklin lead the Constitutional Convention?
Main Idea and Details

	Words Read	−	Number of Errors	=	Words Correct Score
First Read		−		=	
Second Read		−		=	

© Macmillan/McGraw-Hill

At Home: Help your child read the passage, paying attention to the goal at the top of the page.

An American Hero Flies Again
Book 3.2/Unit 6

203

Use the space below to design the words and pictures for a poster. Your poster should be a <u>functional document</u> with information that a good citizen needs in order to do something. For example, you might create a poster advertising an election or a neighborhood meeting to discuss a concern, such as speeding cars or how to best use a vacant lot.

At Home: Ask your child to explain the choice of poster topic and how the poster works as a functional document.

Name _____

A. Many words in English have word parts that come from the Greek language. Write two real English words from each of the Greek roots below. Use a dictionary if you need help.

Greek Root	English Word
1. micro (means small)	_____ _____
2. astro (means star)	_____ _____
3. phon, phone (means sound or voice)	_____ _____
4. therm (means heat)	_____ _____
5. meter, metry (means measuring or measurement)	_____ _____

B. Write sentences using a word you made from each Greek root word.

6. _____

_____

7. _____

_____

8. _____

_____

9. _____

_____

10. _____

_____

© Macmillan/McGraw-Hill

At Home: With your child, come up with examples of words with the Greek roots *auto* and *graph*.

An American Hero Flies Again
Book 3.2/Unit 6
205

Use at least six of the words with the final /ər/ sound in the box to write a letter to the governor of your state. Your letter should express a concern you have as a citizen of your city or town.

summer	September	doctor	lawyer	late	calendar
harbor	never	circular	neighbor	editor	

_____

_____

_____

_____

_____

_____

_____

_____

_____

_____

_____

_____

© Macmillan/McGraw-Hill

At Home: Take turns with your child asking and answering riddles in which each answer has the /ər/ sound at the end of a final unstressed syllable.

Name _____

Read each sentence below and think about the meaning of the underlined vocabulary word. Write your answer in a complete sentence using the vocabulary word.

1. When do you <u>crouch</u>? _____

_____

_____

2. Name two sports where the athletes show <u>grace</u>. _____

_____

_____

3. What <u>official</u> announcement might be presented on television?

_____

_____

4. Name two animals that are <u>sleek</u>. _____

_____

_____

5. When was the last time that you were <u>sleepy</u>, and why? _____

_____

_____

6. Where was the last place that you and your family <u>strolled</u>? _____

_____

_____

7. What does it mean to look <u>pitiful</u>? _____

_____

_____

Think about what you know about how people and animals live together, work together, and help each other. Write three short passages about this theme, each with a different purpose.

Purpose: to inform

_____

_____

_____

_____

Purpose: to entertain

_____

_____

_____

_____

Purpose: to persuade

_____

_____

_____

_____

At Home: Have your child look through newspapers and magazines to find articles, editorials, and stories that show different authors' purposes.

Name _____

As you read *Mother to Tigers*, fill in the Author's Purpose Chart.

Clues

↓

Author's Purpose

How does the information you wrote in this Author's Purpose Chart help you
monitor comprehension in *Mother to Tigers*?

 At Home: Have your child use the chart to retell the story.

Mother to Tigers • Book 3.2/Unit 6 ◇209◇

As I read, I will pay attention to phrasing and intonation.

	When Gerald was fourteen, he got a job in a pet shop in London. At
15	age twenty he got an even better job. He was hired as a student zookeeper
30	at the Whipsnade Zoo in London. Animals were bred and raised there.
42	Gerald learned everything he could about zoo work. He learned what
53	to feed the animals. He learned how to groom and care for them.
66	He also studied how the animals behaved. He wrote notes about them.
78	He was most interested in animals that were in danger of extinction. He
91	hoped someday that he could help save these endangered animals.
101	"I knew exactly what I was going to do," he later wrote. "I was going
116	to have my own zoo."
121	When Durrell turned twenty-one he inherited some family money. He
131	decided to use the money to go on safari in Africa. He wanted to find rare
147	animals and bring them back to English zoos.
155	In 1947 he left with a friend for British Cameroons in West
166	Africa. 167

Comprehension Check

1. What did Gerald learn as a student zookeeper? **Summarize**

2. What did Gerald want to do? **Main Idea and Details**

	Words Read	−	Number of Errors	=	Words Correct Score
First Read		−		=	
Second Read		−		=	

© Macmillan/McGraw-Hill

 At Home: Help your child read the passage, paying attention to the goal at the top of the page.

Name _____

**Write a short fable that teaches a lesson. Include
personification in your fable. Maybe the sun or moon will
talk to an animal in your fable. Maybe two animals
will work together to solve a problem. Ask a partner to
identify the lesson, or moral, of your fable.**

_____

_____

_____

_____

_____

_____

_____

_____

_____

_____

_____

_____

_____

_____

At Home: Have your child draw a picture that personifies an
animal or an object, such as a talking tree.

Name _____

A. Make as many words as you can out of the words in the box by adding the suffix -y or -ly. Remember that for words that end in e, drop the e before adding the -y suffix. For words that end in a single consonant, double the final consonant.

wave	fun	nice	ice	stick
free	quick	pep	remote	gracious

_____   _____

_____   _____

_____   _____

_____   _____

_____   _____

B. Think of some words and add the -y or -ly suffixes to make new words.

Example: shine + y = shiny

1. _____ + _____ = _____

2. _____ + _____ = _____

3. _____ + _____ = _____

4. _____ + _____ = _____

At Home: Ask your child questions that have answers that include words with the suffix -y or -ly.

© Macmillan/McGraw-Hill

Name _____

A. Add the suffix *-ful*, *-less,* or *-ly* to the words in the box. Write as many words as you can on the lines below.

cloud	peace	pain	wonder	success	play	wise
friend	brave	color	meaning	care	sad	taste

_____   _____   _____

_____   _____   _____

_____   _____   _____

_____   _____   _____

B. Write sentences using words that you formed above. Then underline the words that have suffixes.

1. _____

_____

2. _____

_____

3. _____

_____

4. _____

_____

At Home: Challenge your child to use base words and the words with the suffix *-ful*, *-less* or *-ly* in one sentence.

Mother to Tigers • Book 3.2/Unit 6 213

© Macmillan/McGraw-Hill

Name _____

Answer the questions using the underlined vocabulary word.

1. What might you keep in an <u>enclosure</u>?

_____

_____

2. What is something that is helpful to have in <u>supply</u> before a big storm?

_____

_____

3. What activity could you become <u>involved</u> in that would help animals?

_____

_____

4. What plant or animal would you like to <u>protect</u> the most?

_____

_____

5. What is another word to describe animals that <u>disappear</u> from the world?

_____

_____

6. What animal would you like to <u>capture</u> on film?

_____

_____

7. What is <u>harming</u> the environment?

_____

_____

Home-Grown Butterflies
Book 3.2/Unit 6

Name _____

Read the passage below. Write two different conclusions you can draw about the situation that is described.

It was a beautiful Monday morning and Sharon walked to school thinking of the caterpillar experiment her class was doing in science. She attended homeroom and then went to her science class. When she entered science class, all the other students were staring up at the ceiling. Sharon looked up to see what everyone was looking at. She heard the teacher telling everyone to be very careful where they moved as he closed the windows.

Possible conclusion 1: _____

_____

_____

_____

_____

Possible conclusion 2: _____

_____

_____

_____

_____

At Home: Look through magazines or newspapers for interesting photographs or pictures. Take turns with your child drawing conclusions about a few of them.

Home-Grown Butterflies   215
Book 3.2/Unit 6

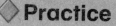
As you read *Home-Grown Butterflies,* fill in the Conclusion Map.

> **Clue**

↓

> **Clue**

↓

> **Clue**

↓

> **Conclusion**

How does the information you wrote in this Conclusion Map help you monitor comprehension in *Home-Grown Butterflies*?

© Macmillan/McGraw-Hill

At Home: Have your child use the chart to retell the story.

Name _____

As I read, I will pay attention to tempo.

	A few years ago, a man in Maryland ordered a pair of live northern
14	snakehead fish from a market in New York City's Chinatown. He
25	wanted to use them to make soup for his sick sister. Snakehead meat is
39	used in soup in China, where he was born.
48	By the time the fish arrived, the man's sister was better. Now he had
62	two live snakeheads on his hands. At first he kept them in an aquarium.
76	When the fish grew too large, he brought them to a pond and set
90	them free.
92	Before long the snakeheads started a colony in the pond. With no
104	natural enemies, their numbers grew. Two years after the man set his
116	fish free, scientists took action. They were able to capture more
127	than a hundred fish, but they didn't know how many more lived in
140	the pond.
142	The scientists were worried. The ecosystem of the pond was in
153	danger. These fish grow up to 3 feet (0.9m) long. Most of their diet
165	is made up of other fish. They could eat all the native fish. 178

Comprehension Check

1. How was a large snakehead colony able to develop in the pond? **Cause and Effect**

2. Why are scientists worried about the growing snakehead population? **Draw Conclusions**

	Words Read	–	Number of Errors	=	Words Correct Score
First Read		–		=	
Second Read		–		=	

© Macmillan/McGraw-Hill

At Home: Help your child read the passage, paying attention to the goal at the top of the page.

Home-Grown Butterflies
Book 3.2/Unit 6 217

Name _____

> **Personification** and **assonance** are literary devices that poets
> use to create pleasing images and sounds. Personification
> gives human characteristics to animals or things. Assonance
> is the repetition of the same or similar middle vowel sound in a
> series of words grouped closely together.

**A. Read each line of poetry. Underline the words that create
assonance. Then write the word for the animal or object that
is being personified.**

1. Its mouth was dripping with a load of slippery soil.

   _____

2. and drinks softly at the faucet

   _____

3. Some stretch out their arms to rest.

   _____

4. Daring pilots, swooping and dipping, then landing with care

   _____

**B. Write two sentences in which an animal or an object has human
characteristics. Include a sound that creates assonance.**

5. _____

   _____

6. _____

   _____

At Home: Help your child describe a few items in your home
in a way that personifies them.

Name _____

**Some words can be used in more than one way. Create a
dictionary entry for a word about the environment that has
more than one meaning, such as *flower*, *soil*, or *hazard*.
Create a dictionary entry for the word. Include:**

- Entry Word

- Parts of Speech

- Numbers for Different Meanings

- Examples of Word in Sentences

_____

_____

_____

_____

_____

_____

_____

_____

_____

_____

_____

© Macmillan/McGraw-Hill

At Home: Tell your child a riddle whose answer is a familiar
word that has more than one meaning. Have your child
guess the word, then tell its other meaning.

In the first column, list the words from the box in which the
first syllable is accented. Mark the syllable break. In the second
column, list the words from the box in which the second syllable
is accented. Mark the syllable break.

attract	swallow	tractor	problem	milkweed	extinct

_____   _____

_____   _____

_____   _____

**Use two of the words from each column in a short paragraph
about the life of butterflies.**

_____

_____

_____

_____

_____

_____

_____

_____

At Home: Scan magazines or newspapers for articles on
the environment. Have your child find several two-syllable
words in one of the articles.

Name _____

Read the story below. Fill in the missing vocabulary words listed in the box.

capture	strolled	supply	disappear
dispute	construction	conversation	equipment
harming	downtown	enclosure	involved
official	historical	interrupted	sleepy

I was sorry that I had disrupted and _____ a

_____ between two speakers. I thought they were having

an argument and _____ about the _____

of some beetles. But they were talking about how people are

_____ these insects. They had a _____ of

them and were keeping them in an _____. They didn't

want the beetles to _____ because they were using

them in a study. It was all legal and _____. I apologized

to the speakers. I said that I would try to remember not to get

_____ in other people's business.

When I left, I walked and _____ _____

through the old _____ district. I like to watch

the _____ that is going on. There is so much big

_____ in the area.

Name _____

A. Choose a word from the box to correctly complete each sentence.

automatically	pitiful	requirements
protect	sway	owners

1. My pet dog looked _____ after getting stuck outside in the snow.

2. There are many difficult _____ for students who want to attend the best school.

3. The security lights _____ turn on when there's any movement outside.

4. The trees began to _____ in the strong wind during the storm.

5. My group wants to _____ the homes of an endangered bird.

6. The _____ of the boat were very upset when it sunk during the storm.

B. Write a short definition for each of the following words.

7. leaky _____

8. seized _____

9. grace _____

10. boasting _____

© Macmillan/McGraw-Hill